Francis W. Morse

Personal Experiences in the War of the Great Rebellion

From December, 1862, to July, 1865

Francis W. Morse

Personal Experiences in the War of the Great Rebellion
From December, 1862, to July, 1865

ISBN/EAN: 9783337116101

Printed in Europe, USA, Canada, Australia, Japan

Cover: Foto ©ninafisch / pixelio.de

More available books at **www.hansebooks.com**

PERSONAL EXPERIENCES

IN THE

War of the Great Rebellion,

FROM

DECEMBER, 1862, TO JULY, 1865.

BY

F. W. MORSE,

BREVET MAJOR AND AIDE DE CAMP.

ALBANY, N. Y.:
PRINTED, BUT NOT PUBLISHED.
1866.

MUNSELL, PRINTER,
ALBANY.

PREFACE.

The following retrospect of my military career was written and printed, but not published, at the solicitation of and exclusively for my immediate family, and not even for my friends. It is not intended for any circulation whatever, and therefore I have the right to claim, and do claim, that it is not amenable to the criticism of any other person, who may happen to see it. It is a simple unstudied narrative, without pretense to style or literary merit of any sort, and does not profess to describe the campaigns and battles in which I was engaged, but only to give an imperfect account of some things which I saw and did, as they now occur to my memory. The only aid which I have had has been a meagre diary of events which I kept during some of the campaigns. I am conscious that almost any one of the thousands of young officers who took part in these stupendous events, could write a better picture of them than I have written, and that the only excuse which I can make for writing and printing this, is the one which I have given, that it is exclusively for the private and indulgent perusal of my own family. They will place some value on it, as it will be a record to show in after years, that they were represented to some extent, though by a boy of only eighteen years of age, in the great work, so dear to them all, of saving their country from ruin.

FRANCIS W. MORSE.

Cherry Valley, July, 1866.

PERSONAL EXPERIENCES

IN THE

WAR OF THE GREAT REBELLION.

COMMISSIONED AND STARTED FOR THE SEAT OF WAR.

On the 15th of December, 1862, His Excellency Governor Morgan of New York commissioned me 1st Lieutenant in the 121st N. Y. Infantry. Accompanying the commission were orders from the adjutant general of the state, to report for duty at the head quarters of my regiment serving in the army of the Potomac. I went home the next day, and by the 22d of the month was en route from New York to Washington, and arrived there on the morning of the 23d, Sunday.

At this time the order requiring all officers to procure passes before going to the front was in force, and I was thereby detained until the day after my arrival, at which time upon application at the provost marshal's office, a very pompous little lieutenant handed me the necessary paper to carry me to the army on the following day. In the evening, through the carelessness of the porter at my hotel, my baggage, containing all my munitions of war, was mistaken for that of a demure minister, and taken to where his had been ordered. The error was not rectified until the day after — too late for me to use the permit which I had received. Whereupon I reported the facts to the provost marshal, and he, considering my reason for remaining over satisfactory, renewed the pass for the next day, making the suggestion that that day would be the proper time for me to leave Washington. The hint was not needed, for I was anxious to join my command. Every thing being ready, I went to the boat on Wednesday morning, and sailed down the Potomac in the rotten transport.

The army was encamped at Fredericksburg, Va., and the means of communication with Washington were by boat to Aquia creek, and thence by rail to Falmouth, the army base of supplies. On landing at Aquia creek, I found to my dismay that my baggage had been left on the dock at Washington. I afterwards recovered a small portion of it. There was one consolation in the loss — I had less to attend to, and before reaching the regiment I had all I could do to attend to myself. The afternoon train composed of box cars, was about to start. I climbed into one and seated myself on a bale of hay, when the train moved at a rate that a tired column of infantry would laugh at, and after two and a half hours, spent in going fifteen miles, stopped at Falmouth.

Arrived at Falmouth.

As I stepped off the train I was ignorant which way to turn, and after turning which way to go to find my regiment. However, as there was no time to lose, I took up my sword, the only article of my wardrobe left, and went to the nearest body of troops in sight. An officer told me that the 121st was in the left grand division, lying about seven miles to the left, pointing with his arm in a bent position, leaving it to my option to look in an easterly, westerly or southerly direction. Thanking him, I started on to find some one who could give me more definite directions, and at last was told by an intelligent chasseur that the 121st was at White Oak Church. By this time darkness had fallen, and a few drops of rain were coming down. I was four miles from my destination. I walked on till eight o'clock, when wet through and exhausted, I determined to find shelter some where for the night, and resume my march in the morning. Seeing a row of large tents a little to the left, I went there, and was received by a captain with the true hospitality which characterizes the Staff corps. He invited me to share his tent and bed with him. I was at the head quarters of General Newton, commanding the 3d division, 6th corps. This was Christmas eve, but I was so tired that I knew nothing except my whereabouts, and soon forgot even that in sleep. On the following morning Captain Ulsoeffer presented me to General Newton and staff. The breakfast to which we soon sat down presented a curious contrast to the one I had had the day before at Willard's hotel, and gave me my first introduction to hard tack.

ARRIVED AT THE REGIMENT.

After breakfast, Captain Ulsoeffer provided me with a horse and orderly, and bidding good morning to the general and staff, I galloped over to the 121st, and immediately went to the tent of the commanding officer, Colonel Emory Upton, and reported myself ready for duty. He received me with military courtesy, and assigned me to a company of my choice, as second officer.

I was now fairly settled and had time to consider the situation. It was dubious. No clothes, cold weather, miserable tent, and little to eat. The romance of a soldier's life vanished.

A SCARE.

The day after my arrival, my company, with several others, was ordered to the picket line to relieve the old guards. As we commenced moving, the rain began to fall, and when we reached the lines I thought we were a woe-begone party to look at. The old pickets marched off, and we took their position. The rain ceased, and was followed by a cold wind. Our line extended to the Rappahannock river opposite Fredericksburg.

At twelve o'clock at night, a dragoon came on the full gallop down the road where I was with my pickets, with the intelligence that the enemy were attempting to lay a pontoon bridge across the river at the city, and that he had dispatches to that effect to General Wheaton, general officer of the division. I doubled the pickets immediately, and was returning to my post, my mind filled with rebels, pontoons and cannon, when General Wheaton with an aid dashed up, and inquiring the way to the river, rode on. In a few minutes another staff officer came up and told me the cause of the alarm. A negro fishing for clams dropped a tub in the river, and the noise had made all this disturbance.

Every thing being quieted I laid down to rest. This was my first night out. With December winds and rain, my position was any thing than comfortable, and in my ignorance of hardships, I thought I could not be in a worse and sadder plight. I lay under some wet pine boughs, thinking of my experience so far, until I fell asleep. At day-break the réveille aroused me. The morning was beautiful; in the distance could be heard the faint notes of the rebel bands playing the air of Dixie, and the rebel pickets loafing in the most comfortable manner under the magnificent trees of the south bank of the river. They were the first "Grey Backs" I had seen. I wondered if such looking vagabonds could fight; but the wonder did not last long in that direction. In the afternoon our pickets were relieved, and we, in our turn, returned to camp.

APPOINTED ADJUTANT.

Late in that afternoon an orderly brought me the "Compliments of Colonel Upton, with the request that I would call at his tent." A little startled, I put on my sabre and obeyed the order. On entering the colonel's tent, I was greeted with the laconic sentence, "Mr. Morse, I wish you to act as adjutant at parade this evening." If I had had more independence I would have requested to be excused, but, as it was, a simple "Yes sir," was my only response, and leaving his tent I went back to mine, not at all relishing the idea of appearing before eight hundred men as a sort of model to be gazed at and criticised, as it seemed to me. However, there was no help for it, and so at six o'clock I paraded out, looking all right I suppose, but feeling very much demoralized. The line was formed, and I commenced operations, and conducted the parade in such a manner, that after it was over the colonel said to me that he would send to the Governor, that evening, a recommendation for me to be appointed to the vacant adjutancy. The promotion was unexpected, and, coming so soon, and after but one trial, was far beyond my hopes. I felt much complimented, as any boy of eighteen years might feel, to be selected out of the thirty-four officers, every one older than I, and of greater experience, for this agreeable and important post.

Dismissed the Service.

With these pleasant feelings I returned to my tent to write home. I found a number of orders from the Secretary of War, and among them one to the effect that:

"First Lieutenant Francis W. Morse of 121st N. Y. V. was dismissed from the service of the United States for being in the city of Washington without proper authority."

By order of the Secretary of War.

My prospects for military glory seemed waning. It was my duty as adjutant to read this order to the regiment. I was astonished and indignant, regarding the order as utterly unjust and insulting. On my stating to Col. Upton the facts out of which it grew, he wrote to the Secretary of War, a letter, of which the following is a copy:

HEAD QUARTERS, 121st REGT. N. Y. VOLS., }
January 12, 1863. }

Brig. Gen. Lorenzo Thomas, Adjutant General U. S. A.

SIR: I have the honor to acknowledge the receipt of special orders, No 5, War Department, January 5th, dismissing First Lieutenant Francis W. Morse of this regiment, "for being in the city of Washington without proper authority." Believing the Department to have been misinformed in his case, I beg leave to present the following statement:

Lieutenant Morse was commissioned by His Excellency Governor Morgan, December 15th, 1862. He arrived in Washington on his way to report for duty, Sunday morning, December 21st. The Provost Marshal's office not being opened on that day, nor on the next day till nine A. M. (an hour after the boat left), he was unable to proceed, for want of a pass, till Tuesday. Tuesday morning, when about to leave for the boat, he found, that through a mistake at his hotel his baggage had been sent to the Baltimore depot. He was unable to procure it before the boat left, and was thus unavoidably detained till another day. He immediately got his pass renewed, and left Washington Wednesday, December 24th, and reported to me for duty. Lieutenant Morse was a very promising and efficient officer, one the service could ill afford to lose, and considering that he was not on duty, and that he used due diligence in repairing to his post, from which he has not been absent for a moment, I trust, so much of the order as dismisses him may be revoked, and that he may be returned to duty.

I am Sir, very respectfully,
Your obedient servant.
EMORY UPTON,
Col. commanding 121st N. Y. Vols.

This letter was endorsed by Generals Bartlett, Brooks, Sedgwick and Franklin, and armed with it, I started for Washington, to demand justice.

Restored.

Through the kindness of General Turner, Judge Advocate of the War Department, the matter was immediately brought before the Secretary of War. The Secretary on learning the facts, at once reinstated me and gave me orders to resume my duty with the regiment.

Upon the restoration of my commission, my first impulse was to find the little lieutenant who falsely reported me, and give him an opportunity to try some passes other than those used in the war department. But I had grown cautious and thought Washington a dangerous place for commissions. After replenishing my wardrobe, I left Washington with a light heart, and sailed down the Potomac with the feelings of a veteran, thinking that this time I was not the raw recruit in search of a regiment. But my self congratulations were premature.

Burnside's Move in the Mud.

On reaching Falmouth, about five P. M., I looked where the army was, and, like the Irishman's flea, it was not there. I saw the end of an immense army train disappearing on a distant hill, and was told that the whole army had moved at day-break on that day, and it was, of course, at that late hour in the afternoon, many miles away.

Nothing could be learned at the depot of the destination of the troops, and so, about six o'clock I started on foot to overtake the train. I wanted to be in at the expected battle. The rain fell in torrents, and as I stepped along in the mud, with the water running down my back, hungry, tired and disgusted, I am afraid my wishes were rather unchristian regarding the little lieutenant, who was the cause of all my trouble. I walked about five miles, and came up to the ammunition trains of

General Franklin. It was dark and raining powerfully. I could not stop, as I thought there would be a battle before morning. I continued walking and inquiring, but nobody knew any thing of Brooks's division. Brigadiers were asking where their brigades were, and major generals looking for their own head quarters. All mixed up. I kept on walking till about nine or ten o'clock wet through, till I came across the train of the 2d brigade 3d division 6th corps, and found they were going to General Newton's division, and so went on with them. At last the roads became so horrible that no farther progress could be made, and they stopped in a swamp. Every thing was so wet that it was out of the question to build a fire, and I had the prospect of standing all night in the mud and rain, with braying mules and swearing teamsters.

My disgust was at its height when an officer rode up, who proved to be the quartermaster of the train. He invited me to eat hard tack, and to make myself as comfortable as possible under one of his wagons. I ate a cracker, and throwing the cape of my coat over my head, laid down in the mud, and as it grew warm, fell asleep.

About four o'clock in the morning orders came to move, but as I was fighting then on my own hook I did not move till seven — and oh, how stiff and cold I felt then. As the rain had not abated during the night, it was impossible for the train to move and I started to find my corps. I had gone about two miles when I saw in one pile twenty-two dead horses, and for miles around army wagons and pontoons stuck in the mud. I saw in one place two hundred and seventy-five men and eight mules attempting in vain to move one pontoon.

After searching all day I found my regiment at Banks's Ford on the Rappahannock. As I reported my return to the Colonel I found him conversing with several general and field officers to whom he presented me, and complimented me upon my alacrity in overcoming the difficulties in my way. The army was mud bound, and already the movement was considered a failure. Infantry could not move; artillery was stuck all along the roads, and every thing was in a complete state of blockade on account of the mud. General Burnside, commanding the army, made the movement in hopes of regaining his military reputation lost at the faulty and bloody battle of Fredericksburg on the 15th of December, 1862; but fortune, through the elements, still frowning on him the plan was abandoned, and orders issued for the troops to return to their former camps. Upton's regiment was in the rear of the corps, and as the columns moved, we received orders to remain at the river as pickets, during the night. I was directed to place two companies in the thicket, on the banks of the river, with as little noise as possible, as the enemy were on the other side. At this place the river was but a few yards in width. Every thing was successfully done, and by four A. M. we were on the march to join the main columns. By five P. M. on the 20th we reached our old camps, and resumed the duties of troops in permanent quarters.

BURNSIDE RELIEVED, HOOKER MADE GEN. IN CHIEF.

General Burnside was soon relieved from command and General Joseph Hooker assigned to the army as commander-in-chief. Immediately upon General Hooker's advent, the army was divided into corps, divisions and brigades. Three divisions were made in each corps, three brigades in each division, and three to six regiments in a brigade. My regiment was in the 2d brigade, General Bartlett, 1st division, General Brooks, and 6th corps, Major General Sedgwick commanding. The whole corps numbered about twenty thousand men.

Until this time I scarcely had had any opportunity to become much acquainted with my fellow officers, or with the duties of my new position. As

Colonel Upton had an extensive acquaintance in the army, and generally I accompanied him on his rides, but a short time elapsed before I saw many familiar faces in each corps, and among the many regiments and staffs formed pleasant friendships. There is nothing like hardship and privation to bring out all the traits of man, good or bad, and the army of the Potomac had been sufficiently tried, to develop many characters of unselfishness and true nobility, among whom I made many friends. I joined the army during the darkest days of the war, immediately after the poorly conducted campaign in Maryland, and the terribly bloody and wicked battle of Fredericksburg, but the men were not disheartened, nor the spirits of the troops depressed. General Hooker adopted such firm and systematic modes of discipline, that early in the winter the troops were in a condition never before equaled. The army of the Potomac was composed of the 1st, 2d, 3d, 5th, 6th, 11th, and 12th corps, each corps having a distinguishing badge. The 6th corps had the Greek cross. As soon as the army was fairly organized, drills, parades and reviews were of daily occurrence. Infantry, cavalry and artillery were brought to the highest point of drill. Our camp was not in a very romantic place, nor were my surroundings adapted to make me very frolicsome, so that in a quiet way I passed my first month under canvas.

In February I applied for a leave of absence, and went home, but remained there only two or three days. Though not at all fascinated with the army, I had a great desire to be back with my corps, taking part in events which were making the greatest of military histories. Little did I know of the dangers, privations and annoyances I should pass through before I again returned home. I was promptly back on the day my leave expired, and resumed my duties. My experience was not seasoned with any of those episodes which afterwards lent so much interest to my military life. Tied down to an infantry regiment, I was of no account outside of the brigade, and had only hard work, hard knocks, and hard tack. As spring approached, preparations were made to open the campaign of 1863. The army numbered one hundred and twenty thousand men. We knew the coming struggle would be desperate and sanguinary, for General Lee, commanding the rebel army, had about an equal number of men. Ammunition, rations, clothing, and equipments of all kinds were rapidly accumulating. At length all leaves were stopped, and the weather being fair, we looked daily for orders to " break camp."

Campaign of Chancellorsville.

By the 27th of the month the country was considered to be in a sufficiently settled condition to warrant the opening of the campaign. General Hooker promulgated a patriotic and stirring order, accompanying which were orders for the army to be in readiness to move. The army was encamped on the line of the Rappahannock, and about one mile from it, forming a front of nearly eight miles. Lee's army was encamped on the south side in a manner so as to confront ours at all points. On the afternoon of the 27th, the 6th corps broke camp, and moved down to the gaps in Stafford Heights, half a mile from the river, there to await the coming of night, so as to cross the river under cover of darkness. The disposition of the several corps was as follows: the 2d, 3d, 5th, 11th and 12th, were to move up the river eleven miles, and to cross at Banks's Ford; the 6th to cross at the city of Fredericksburg at Franklin's crossing, and the 1st corps to cross one mile below at Seddon's crossing.

As my experience in the battle of Chancellorsville did not of course extend out of my own corps, I shall only mention its movements. As we were in the deep ravines of Stafford Hills, waiting for night to come, a cold drizzling rain fell, and with it came a thick fog. At length night approached, and while waiting for the pontoons to be brought, I had ample time for reflection. Here was the same place where five months before the corps had met with a terrible repulse, trying to do the same thing that we were to attempt that night. But bitter experience had taught our generals to adopt a different mode of attack. On the opposite side of the river were the rebel pickets in strong force, and necessarily we would have to cross in their fire. The engineers were very late in bringing up the pontoons; it was now two o'clock, and there was but little time to lose. While we were waiting, a staff officer rode up and told us our brigade with Russell's, was to cross first, and establish a footing on the other side. At three A. M., the boats were ready, forty-five men were to go in each boat, pull across, and upon reaching the opposite bank to spring ashore and charge the enemy's works. As we pushed the boats in the river, the rebels opened a brisk musketry fire, and a few men fell; but we were in for it and across we went, jumped on the shore, and by a vigorous assault captured the rebel works and quite a number of prisoners. The way was now open, and at daybreak, the remainder of the corps, after laying down the pontoon bridge, crossed and took position on our right and left. The heavy guns firing in the direction of Banks's Ford, told us that the rest of the army was meeting with stubborn resistance. On the afternoon of the 28th, the 1st corps made its crossing below, suffering the loss of a few men. So far every thing had admirably succeeded, and we had high hopes of a speedy and splendid victory.

This affair was my first, and a good initiation it was; a kind of a storming party affair, and as it was successful I was very well satisfied for having been in it.

The 28th, 29th and 30th of April, and 2d of May, were passed in continual skirmishing to put the army in position for the grand battle. In our front the force of the enemy was supposed to be inferior to ours, but the disastrous rout of the 11th corps, on the 2d, enabled General Lee to send from Chancellorsville a force largely to outnumber us. In the evening of the 2d, we knew every thing was prepared for us to open the battle on the morning following.

Battle of Salem Chapel and Chancellorsville.

At three A. M., Sunday, the 3d of May, 1863, the réveille awoke us, the moon was brightly shining, and our long lines of battle moved out on the plain to await the breaking of day. Batteries and battalions were ready. As the sun rose we marched out on the beautiful plain of Fredericksburg, in full view of the enemy, who were entrenched on Maries Hills and all their guns turned on our columns. At 4.40, the artillery opened. Eighty guns vomited out their contents, and never shall I forget the astonishment of my ears as, for the first time to them, the solid shot, shell and bolts yelled, shrieked and plowed about. Men and horses fell, cannons and limbers blew up. Still the batteries continued their unearthly noise and destruction. At six o'clock we were moved forward three quarters of a mile into Deep Run, and there were under cover. Staying there but a few minutes we moved to the left in support of Heximer's battery, actively engaged with a battery of the enemy about twelve hundred yards off. The men found protection from the rebel shot by lying flat on their faces; but as Colonel Upton remained mounted, I did also, though thinking every shell especially fired at me. The artillery was now doing most of the fighting, though the infantry was drawing closer to the enemy. At eleven o'clock, the light division, General Pratt, was ordered to charge the hill. Advancing in three lines of battle, with colors flying and guns glistening in the sun, they looked splendidly, and in firm unbroken lines stormed the works, rushing through clouds of shell and balls. Soon we saw the United States flag floating over the most difficult portion of the works, and, with cheers from the troops below, we marched through the city and out on the Richmond road up to Maries Hill. There we found the light division resting on their guns and laurels, the most self satisfied set of men I ever saw.

The rebels had retreated four miles, taking a strong position at Salem Chapel. At two P. M., we made the "noon halt." In our mess hamper were bread, ham, and two bottles of champagne. Scarcely were we seated, when an aid came to us with orders to fall in — putting back the champagne much to our grief, we mounted our horses. As we marched out on the road and were fairly under way, a twenty pound shell whizzed over our heads, taking the compliments of a rebel battery to Williston, commanding Battery D, 2nd Artillery. Williston sent his regards back in a similar manner, and between those two attentive parties, we were in somewhat of a predicament. Rapidly our lines moved forward, halting at the edge of a large wood. Batteries were put in position. Skirmishing had reopened with vigor. At four P. M., I carried the order from General Brooks to General Bartlett, to advance his line, and then joined my regiment. I had undergone the ordeal of artillery well enough; now came the trial of charging infantry.

The 121st held the centre of the brigade. We advanced in the woods, when suddenly a fire of thirty-six hundred muskets opened chiefly upon our regiment. The whole line to me seemed to have been blown away; my horse was shot through the neck, but was not totally disabled. The colors shot down, six bearers picked them up, each in his turn to die. Our men still pressed on until within twenty feet of the rebel redoubts, and then opened fire. As we halted, my saddle was struck by a ball; at the same time my horse was killed outright by a bullet going through his head, and fell instantly. When I struck on the ground I was in a sitting position. Upton's horse was killed at the same time. We pressed the first line of rebels back on the second, and that being the stronger, held its ground with great firmness. No mortal could stay and live where we were, and the line moved back and retreated in confusion. Seeing the colors lying on the ground, I picked them up and started for the rear, but impeded by them, by my big spurs and sabre, I fell down three times, and did not get out of the woods till the rebels were close on our heels. Meeting General Bartlett in the field, I gave him the colors, and started for the regiment; when suddenly my leg, just above the ankle, was struck by a ball, and down I fell. The leg immediately grew stiff, I could not stand on it, and the pain was excruciating. Looking back I saw the rebel lines advancing but a few yards off, and felt their bullets whizzing apast. Springing on my left leg, by the aid of my sabre I hobbled to the regiment. The men rallied, formed into lines again, and repulsed the advancing enemy. As I saw the 121st together again, I could scarcely believe my eyes — but a handful left. Out of 452 who entered, two hundred and ninety were left in the woods, dead, wounded and missing.

We were back in our old position, and the rebels in theirs, with the dead and wounded of both sides between the lines. My leg was very painful and much swollen; the thickness of my large boot saved me from a wound; as it was, I had suffered a severe contusion. Captain Richards, of General Bartlett's staff, gave me a horse. The night was passed in a continuous roll of artillery and musketry, and on Monday the battle was resumed, resulting in great loss to the rebels, and we holding our ground. Tuesday night, General Sedgwick moved the corps up to Chancellorsville, and there joined the remainder of the army.

The entire battle was now considered lost. Hooker had not succeeded, and therefore our corps could not effectively perform its work. General Hooker deemed it advisable to recross the river to the north side, and abandon the campaign. On the 6th, the crossing was commenced, and attended with great peril, as the river had risen four feet. The pontoon bridge was in a very dilapidated way, and was continually struck by the shells of the enemy.

At length the army was across in camp, each man congratulating himself upon his escape. On the morning of the 8th we marched back to our old camp, filled with feelings of sadness and amazement at the unexpected turn affairs had taken. The army was not whipped nor demoralized; General Hooker could have recrossed the river, and fought another battle with as good chances of success as on the 27th of April. By the 9th, we were in our old camp settled. Truly the sight was a sad one; a large portion of the tents was deserted, the former inmates dead or wounded; there were no loud laughs heard, as each one had a comrade to mourn for. At dress parade when once my voice had to be loud and strong, now I scarcely needed to speak above a natural tone to be heard through the length of the line. Four officers, my kindest friends, were dead or wounded. As soon as we were settled we commenced to make out our reports of the killed, wounded and missing, and loss of property. Letters by hundreds were received from friends and relations of the soldiers inquiring after the fate of friends. The only answer was lists of casualties, which I sent to the papers. Our loss was ninety-two killed, one hundred and seventy wounded, and thirty missing. The loss in the corps was about six thousand, and in the brigade seventeen hundred.

Summer had come; peach, pear and apple trees were in blossom, and foliage of every description in full growth. To look across the river at the beautiful plains and hills of Fredericksburg, one could scarcely believe that such a gigantic battle had there been fought, in which thirty thousand men had been placed *hors de combat*, and that hundreds of killed were peacefully lying beneath those trees that looked so lovely. Amidst drills, parades and reviews, we soon forgot the unpleasant part of the battle of Chancellorsville — all but the 11th corps, and that was an object of derision until it finally left the army. On the 15th of May, the time of six New York regiments had expired; but there were men in each whose time of service had not expired, and these were transferred to the 121st, making up our loss in battle. The usual routine of camp life was resumed, and we were anxiously waiting to see the further movements of General Hooker or General Lee.

Third Crossing of the Rappahannock.

On the 2d of June, Howe's 2d Division was ordered to cross the river at Franklin's crossing, supported by the remainder of the corps. The crossing was effected, as on the former occasions, and once more we were on the offensive. About midnight on the 3d, our brigade moved out on the plain one mile, and in line of battle all the regiments laid down to sleep. The Vermont brigade came up armed only with shovels, and silently commenced digging a few yards in our front. The forms of the men in relief against the sky, seemed phantoms preparing graves for the 2,700 men there sleeping. With the steady pick pick of the spades in my ears I fell asleep, and at daybreak when the troops stood to arms, we saw to our surprise the most complete line of entrenchments that skillful engineers could make. We immediately occupied the works, batteries were brought up and put in position, and then we kept quiet, waiting for something to happen.' During all our operations, General Lee had moved a large portion of his army northward, leaving but a corps in our front, with orders for it to join him when we withdrew. As soon as General Hooker knew General Lee's movement, he started in pursuit, leaving the 6th corps as rear guard.

In the night of the 14th the whole corps was withdrawn, and on the day following, with the 6th corps commenced

The Campaign and Battle of Gettysburg.

On the 15th of June, the "line of the Rappahannock" was abandoned, and we commenced our march. Just before we left, we mounted a 100-pounder Parrott that President Lincoln had sent to the army. There was one battery of Whitworth's guns still in the rebel works nearly three miles off. Our big gun was fired once. The immense shell whizzed and whirled through the air, until finally we saw its thin white smoke as it burst. Immediately after there was a terrible explosion, and vast columns of smoke and dust were thrown in the air. The shell had struck a caisson, and blown it to pieces; the recoil dismounted our 100-pounder, and it was sent back to Washington to Mr. Lincoln with a history of its exploit.

If my first battle had been one of defeat, and I had joined the army at the most gloomy period, I was soon to be a participator in a most brilliant and desperate battle, and in a victory upon which the fate of the war depended.

General Lee had a second time invaded Maryland and Pennsylvania. His infantry, cavalry and artillery were ahead of us several days, and there was not an obstacle in his front to oppose his march. His army had been strongly reinforced; his troops considered themselves invincible, able to kick the army of the Potomac from the Potomac to the Hudson; while our army with a loss in battle of seventeen thousand men, and regiments leaving whose time of service had expired, was left in somewhat straitened circumstances to commence a vigorous campaign.

General Hooker's dispositions of the army on the march were made so that by moving on interior lines he could keep even with General Lee, and at the same time cover Washington from any attempt that might be made to capture it. The exact destination of General Lee was unknown to us, and until we saw a New York paper, we were ignorant of his whereabouts. As we were the rear guard of the army, we were very much annoyed by the guerillas, who were bold and ugly. Our annoyances were frequent, and on the first days of the campaign the danger was so great, that any moment a ball might be expected as a messenger of promotion to the other world.

With the campaign of Gettysburg commenced my marching. Night and day we kept it up. Occasionally the daily marches were very long; twenty to twenty-five miles. The heat and dust were intolerable; the sun affected the men so that many a poor fellow fell down dead from sunstroke, and whole companies would fall out in a state of complete exhaustion. I remember the hottest day we had, about five thousand men in the corps were lying in the woods on account of the heat. I thought I was as liable as any one to be sunstruck, and therefore bound a wet rag around my neck and put leaves in my cap, and then discovered that the sun was just setting and the air becoming quite cool. That night all that the Colonel, Lieutenant Colonel and I had to satisfy an appetite made by an abstinence from food for twenty-four hours, was one can of peaches. About the middle of June, we reached the Potomac and crossed on pontoons at Edward's ferry. From the red clay lands of Virginia, we stepped on the beautiful green fields of Maryland. I think as each soldier threw a look back at Virginia, there was no blessing in his expression. The cavalry had now commenced to skirmish with the enemy. Rumors by the thousands came to us concerning the enemy and our forces. The guerillas continued to pay us little attentions, and kept us supplied with little adventures, that served very well to relieve the monotony of long dusty marches.

In the evening of the 30th of June, we reached Manchester, Md. Lee's army was in Pennsylvania 120,000 strong, ours was but 58,000, and partially acting on the offensive. Hooker was relieved, and of his successor the army knew but little. The terrible odds against us, the all important issues at stake, known to every man in the army, served only to nerve each one to stand up and die fighting. One not connected with the army at that time, can neither know nor appreciate the sentiments that possessed the hearts of the men. The battle of Gettysburg demonstrated the fact that the army of the Potomac would be annihilated rather than defeated on its own ground.

At eight P. M., the 1st of July, we resumed the march, our division taking the lead. All night long without halt, worn out, eyes aching from want of sleep, faint from want of nourishment, we marched along, but without a murmur, or complaint. The heat was deathly, dust filled our throats; but still the march was kept up all night, with no time to rest, no time to eat, no time for any thing but suffering. The faces of the troops were haggard and distorted by fatigue, their feet swollen and their shoes in consequence thrown away; but with all this there was a look of determination in their eyes which plainly spoke on the two days following. Twice during that night I fell off my horse while asleep. At twelve o'clock on the morning of the 2d of July, after a march of thirty-six miles in eighteen hours, we moved in sight of the battle field of Gettysburg, marching to the tune of one hundred guns; but not a straggler, nor a recreant was in the 6th corps. Each man was there with his musket and sixty rounds of cartridges, anxious to send his message of defiance to that proud army of rebels.

As we halted in line of battle, we listened to the fearful attack of Longstreet on the 5th corps directly in our front. Those awful steady rolls of musketry made our hearts beat quick, and inspired us with anxiety to relieve our comrade corps. At last, when the roar of shot and shell, canister and musketry had become hideous, an aid-de-camp came up on full gallop from army head-quarters, with orders for us to engage the enemy. But a few hundred yards in front were 30,000 of the best troops of the rebel army, commanded by their ablest general; with guns firmly clenched our lines moved steadily forward, our gallant colonel rode in front of our regiment, and I at his side wondering if I would be called for now; but we had barely got under steady fire, when the enemy retreated, leaving us in possession of all the ground we wanted, and all we could conveniently attend to. Night came; we were on "Little round Top"—what we had endured during the past two days soon had full effect upon us. We dropped where we stood, and the men instantly fell in a deep dead sleep. I rolled off my horse, and resting my head upon the body of Captain Casler was soon forgetful of battles. At three A. M. on the 3d, the picket firing was so sharp as to awaken me, and then the groans of the wounded and dying kept me awake until the whole corps were under arms. As I rose from my uncomfortable bed, my bones were sore and flesh bruised by the stones. Around us were the dead of both armies, and several hundred yards in our front were the frowning lines and batteries of Longstreet. Our position was wonderfully favorable. No place could have been fitter for artillery, for the inside lines of manœuvering, for reinforcing, for the cover of walls, and of natural defenses. During the early morning of the 3d, cannonading and musketry firing had been continuous.

About ten A. M. the firing on the east side and

every where on our line ceased. A silence fell on the battle field. Our army cooked, ate and slumbered. The rebel army moved one hundred and twenty guns to the west, and there massed Longstreet's and Hill's corps to hurl them upon really the weakest portion of our lines. At eleven, twelve and one o'clock, all was still. Under the shade cast by big trees lay Upton, the Major and I, on a poncho, wondering what next would happen. I turned to Major Mather and remarked we would attack, or be attacked before night. Scarcely were the words out of my mouth when a Whitworth ball hurled over our heads. We sprang up to see whence it came, and as we left the poncho a shell just grazed it; ten seconds sooner we would have been among the unfortunate.

In less than two minutes the fire of the rebel one hundred and twenty guns was directed on the right of our line. The air was full of the most complete artillery prelude to an infantry battle that was ever exhibited. Every size and form of shell known to American and British gunnery, screeched, moaned and wrathfully flew over the ground. From three to six in a second constantly bursting and screaming over our line made a perfect hell of fire that amazed the old veterans. Not a straggler, not an orderly, not an ambulance was to be seen on that plain ten minutes after the fire opened. One hundred and twenty guns were trying to sweep from the field every battery we had in position to resist their prepared infantry attack, and to clear away the slight defenses behind which our infantry were waiting. Forty minutes, fifty minutes were counted on watches that ran too slowly. The air grew thicker and fuller and more deafening with the howling and whirling of these infernal missiles. Time slugglishly moved on, and when after an hour and a half there was a lull, we knew the rebel infantry was to charge. Splendidly they did their work. Picket's division in three lines of battle came first with guns at "right shoulder shift." Longstreet's corps came as supports at the usual distance. With war cries and savage yells they rushed across the plain in perfect order up to the very muzzles of our guns, which tore lanes through them as they came, and they met men who were their equals in spirit and superiors in strength. The rebels were over our works; they had cleaned cannoniers and horses from one of our batteries, and were turning it upon us as the bayonet drove them back. From the exhaustion of their ammunition every battery of ours on the east was relieved except Cowan's of New York. His service of grape and canister was awful; it enabled our line, outnumbered two to one, first to beat back Longstreet, charge upon him and take many prisoners. So terrible was our artillery and musketry fire, that Armstead's brigade was checked in its charge, and stood reeling; all his men dropped their muskets and crawled on their hands and knees under this stream of fire, and on making signs of surrendering were permitted to come into our lines. They passed by us scarcely noticed, and went down the road to the rear.

The grand charge of Ewell, solemnly sworn to and carefully prepared, had failed. The rebels returned to their former lines and opened anew the storm of shot and shell from their one hundred and twenty guns. Those who were there will never forget the dodging and running of the Butternuts when they were under their friend's fire. Again did that terrible tempest of iron hurl itself upon us; our batteries replied with equal fury; and the air again was full of fragments of iron. During this period some of our batteries, whose ammunition was exhausted, retired, and this was thought by General Lee, to be the most favorable time again to advance his columns. The rebels saw the batteries withdrawn, but did not see the reserve artillery taking the vacated places. In three lines of battle the enemy charged for a second time to break our lines; but the annihilating fire of our fresh batteries, and counter charge of our infantry, completely destroyed the assaulting columns.

At four P. M. the fire of the enemy had ceased, and we were the victors—having gained the battle under the most adverse and trying circumstances. The experience of the tried and veteran soldiers of the army of the Potomac tells of no such desperate conflict as was in progress in the third of July, 1863. The cannonading of Chancellorsville and Malvern was mere pastime compared to that of this day. The ground was thick with rebel dead mingled with our own. Thousands of prisoners were taken; twenty-eight thousand stands of small arms together with a quantity of artillery fell into our hands. General Lee's aggregate losses were nearly forty thousand men during the campaign, and General Meade's total loss killed, wounded and missing was twenty-three thousand. Immediately, upon Lee's terrible and final repulse in the afternoon of the 3d, he commenced his retreat.

Pursuit of General Lee.

At four A. M. on the 4th, the 6th corps was made the advance, and ordered to give the rebels a vigorous pursuit. As we advanced we marched over hundreds of dead bodies of our late enemies, scarcely buried. Dismounted cannons, broken down ambulances and straggling rebels plainly showed the line of retreat. The trees and fences for miles in rear were cut up by musket and cannon balls. All along the rebels had filled the immense Pennsylvania barns with their wounded, and large encampments of rebel hospital tents were in the fields, and thus all the severely wounded of the rebel army were left to our tender mercies — General Lee being well aware that we did not act toward our enemy in the barbarous way the high minded sons of the south did to theirs.

In the afternoon of the 4th our advance struck the skirmishers of the rebel rear guard, our batteries were formed in line of battle, and we moved forward under a raking shell fire, pressed back their advanced line upon the reserves, and then drove the whole force into the gaps of the mountains at Fairfield, five miles from Gettysburgh, and here we went into camp for the night.

Before day-break on the morning of the 5th General Sedgwick sent Colonel Kent of his staff with a squadron of cavalry to our regiment, with orders for us to accompany Kent out on the Fairfield road on a reconnoissance. Our lines were deployed, and advanced at a brisk rate. About 9 A. M. we came in sight of a rebel line of battle and attacked them. I was with the front of the line that rested on the crest of a small hill. The balls flew around, over and under me, keeping me winking, dodging and squirming for full an hour. I was a good mark for the enemy, being the only officer mounted in that part of the line. At length the left of the line was attacked by the rebels with great spirit. I rapidly rode there and found Colonel Upton; he told me to ride to General Sedgwick and tell him the situation according to my knowledge of affairs. I found the general sitting on a stump, his staff seated about him, and recounted to him all that had transpired. When I finished, he very quietly asked me, how I knew any thing about it as my regiment was not in the party. I answered, it was, and that accounted for my information. Turning to Colonel Kent the general said, it was the 119th Pennsylvania ordered out, and not the 121st New York. Kent's confusion was great, and my indignation greater, to think my precious life had been exposed by mistake all the morning, when some Pennsylvania adjutant might as well have been in the same place; and from the way the natives of the Key Stone State had treated us, the life of one of them had but little value in our eyes. By the time I returned to our line, it had ceased firing and was resting; the enemy had retired in confusion, and our object was gained.

In the morning of the 6th, the whole corps was in motion, moving forward ten miles, when we came in sight of the entire rebel wagon train. We advanced in one line of battle, batteries advancing in our intervals by battery. At length our batteries opened fire with solid shot from a hill nearly fourteen hundred yards from the rebels. We soon saw the Gray Backs skipping and jumping about to get away from this fire. Every moment we expected the order to charge, but it did not come, and from that day to this I cannot imagine why eight or ten thousand men were not ordered to the attack. We would have captured trains and cannon, beside recovering hundreds of our men taken prisoners.

Gradually Lee gained upon us in his retreat. For ten days the 6th corps did not come in contact with the rebel rear guard, and until nearly the middle of July there was but little done but marching. Lee had reached the Potomac at Williamsport, and the river was so much swollen by the rain that he could not ford it, and for the want of pontoons, he was forced to entrench himself until he could construct bridges in sufficient numbers to cross large bodies of men at once.

At this point the 121st was actively engaged in the same manner as at Fairfield. My good fortune still kept with me, and from that affair I escaped untouched. Through his timidity, or from some other unknown reason, General Meade did not make an attack on the enemy at this place, which, if it had been done, would probably have resulted in the rout of Lee's army, or for a time placed it *hors de combat*. General Lee put his army in safety across the river, and resumed his retreat. The 6th corps moved down the river, and crossed at Berlin, six miles below Harper's Ferry, again meeting the rebels at Funkstown, and after considerable skirmishing, succeeded in driving them entirely out of our reach. After the 25th of July the army was not engaged with the exception of the cavalry, to any extent. Lee effected his retreat without suffering any further losses, and made his encampments on the south side of the Rapidan; the 6th corps encamping in and around Warrenton.

Camp in Summer.

Six miles from Warrenton is a little place called New Baltimore, where our brigade was encamped as kind of a flank guard for the army. Now came our recompense for the two previous months of toil and danger. In the month of August, camped on fine land with all the fruit growing around we could wish for, in quick communication with Washington, and paymasters regular in their visits, we were perfectly contented. Drills, reviews and parades were resumed, and as Chancellorsville had been, so Gettysburg was in its turn soon forgotten in anticipating coming events.

Again the dull camp life became wearisome. The first episode was an execution, the first I ever had seen. I went partially out of curiosity and partly because I was obliged to go. The prisoner was seated on his coffin in a wagon; the division formed in three sides of a square; the wagon containing the condemned was drawn around the inside of the square, a dirge being played; at length the wagon halted at the open side; the coffin was placed on the ground, and the prisoner blind-folded was seated upon it. At the signal from the provost marshal ten balls pierced the unhappy man's breast; he was then laid on his back, and a quick time march played while the entire division marched past the corpse in review.

GUERILLAS.

About the middle of the month I was afflicted in the same way that the damsel in *Pilgrim's Progress* was, that is, "I ate too much fruit," and at one time thought the fruit would be too much for me. One night before I was able to sit up, I was lying in my tent thinking of things in general, when suddenly pop went a pistol, and instantly thirty more spit out their wicked noise. Speedily the whole brigade was out. The firing was in the direction of General Bartlett's head quarters. The men rushed up to the general's in their night uniform, with muskets in their hands. We had been attacked by a company of guerillas, but the rascals were driven off with a loss on our side of two, and in the words of the newspaper correspondent, "that of the enemy's must have been much greater."

An Expedition of 121st.

On the 25th of the month a little expedition was proposed, viz: to divide the regiment in two battalions; one commanded by the colonel, the other by the lieutenant colonel; to take separate roads, and go out in the country for provisions (though at the time we had more than the men could eat), and for guerillas, and of course any thing else that might turn up. Early on the 26th, in light marching order, three hundred men in each division commenced their march. I went with the detachment under the lieutenant colonel. At two o'clock on the morning of the 27th, we reached the town of Salem, a place of six hundred inhabitants.

Immediately we put a line of pickets around the town; with one company, I went to the upper part of the town, and there waited until day-break to commence operations. At day-light, I moved in one end of the fated place and the lieutenant colonel in the other. At the right of us, the poor people were terror-stricken and tried to escape; but that line of pickets made the town a cage, and nothing could be done but quietly submit. Until we were fairly at their doors, the people did not know there was a Yankee within forty miles of them; but we had arrived, and struck terror to their hearts. The town was divided into sections, and one assigned to the especial care of each officer for him to inspect for arms, provisions, &c. We knew well enough that the people were just as innocent of having arms, as we were of having consciences, and not much time was lost before we found that provisions were not so plentiful as they might have been. However, after I had examined one lady's house, frightened her daughter, who was in bed, most out of her wits, I said I would be happy to breakfast with her, and hoped I would see her family in a dress not quite so regardless of appearances as I left them in.

Things went on very pleasantly, and I think we would have gained the affections of the whole community by our little attentions, if we had not arrested and carried off all the fathers, sons and lovers. At 4 p. m., we left the town, without spoils, except men. As we marched up the main street my risibles were sorely tested; in our midst was a procession baffling description, negroes performing all kinds of delightful evolutions, the sullen, long haired Virginian looking ugly, and an old minister trying to resign himself to his fate. Though we laughed to our heart's content, they could not see where the laugh came in. With the tramp of a magnanimous and victorious foe we moved gradually out of town, and halted two miles from it. I thought I would like to say a few words to the minister; he told me it was Sunday (the first I knew of it), and also that he was to preach that morning. After a few minutes talk with him I thought the people of Salem should bless us for relieving them of such an old pest.

At sunset the march was continued and kept up until two o'clock in the afternoon of the day following, when we reached the truly magnificent estate of John A. Washington. We stayed there long enough to dine, and thinking the United States wanted a few more horses, we took all there were on the place and moved on. At one A. M., on the next day, or rather night, we reached our old camp, with prisoners and horses, in safety; the horses were turned into the quartermaster's department, and the prisoners allowed to return home, we thinking a little walk of thirty-eight miles would improve their dispositions. The negroes would not return, but stayed with us. We had a great deal of fun, and I have no doubt that the people of Salem to this day remember the invasion of August, 1863.

Marching.

Until the 12th of September nothing of consequence occurred. On the 12th, orders suddenly came for the brigade to withdraw its pickets and move to Warrenton. The corps had already left Warrenton; our brigade was the rear guard, and the 121st in the rear of all. We entered Warrenton at 11 P. M. This town was deserted by troops; every house and street looked desolate. We moved through the city, and encamped in the suburbs on the Fayetteville road. While the corps was in Warrenton nearly every young lady had lost her heart to some officer, and the movement being so sudden the young sons of Mars did not have time to say good-bye. So at day-break all the young F. F. V's came to us. I was riding through the streets with some orders, when I was assailed with questions: Do you know Major — or Captain — or Colonel so and so? I said yes to every thing, and was made the bearer of messages that never got to the intended recipient. Well might some of the 6th corps men say, "If this is war may there never be peace." The morning of the 13th we moved down to the Rapidan and relieved the 2d corps. While on the bank of that river I was a witness to a second execution; seeing anything of the kind once ought to be sufficient for any one. General Lee now made some new demonstrations towards Washington, which rendered General Meade uneasy on that city's account, and he immediately commenced a retrograde march: day and night we marched in that cool season of the year, October; the suffering from cold in the nights, from hunger and fatigue, was too much for me now to realize. From the Rapidan to Centerville heights was one forced march. Warren's 2d corps met the enemy at Bristol station, and captured five guns, and two hundred and fifty prisoners. That was the only fighting the infantry had, and with the exception of Kilpatrick's cavalry operations, was all the powder burnt on this stampedy march. While on Centerville heights just in the act of sitting down to a hot good dinner some of "*Lee's Miserables*" opened a heavy cannonade at Bull Run, and General Meade fearing trouble at Chantilly, sent us down there post haste, leaving our inner man in a somewhat demoralized condition. We reached Chantilly, made entrenchments, put batteries in position, felled acres of woods in our front, stood to arms all the time, and I do not believe, and did not then, that there was a rebel soldier within twenty miles of us. After staying there three days we returned to Centerville through Bull Run, and went down the Gainsville road to New Baltimore.

At New Baltimore we met the infantry of General Ewell's rear guard, and wasted enough ammunition on them to enable the Fenians to take Canada, and then permitted them peacefully to retire to the south side of the Rappahannock river. We reached Warrenton on the 24th day of October, having been on a campaign of over five weeks, and made a circle of two hundred miles, or in other words, completed the "grand rounds." The corps moved two miles from Warrenton, pitched tents, and resumed drills and every thing else incidental to camp life. By this time the evenings were long, and with nothing to do, we were at our wits' end for amusement. While there are cards, whisky and wines in an army they will be the ruling pleasures. My dislike to cards had a good trial, and not being copper-lined

I could not drink commissary whisky, so that I had an idle, tedious time till it was interrupted by the glorious achievement which I have now the pleasure to record.

Battle of Rappahannock Station. Promotion.

On the night of the sixth of November, I was at the 6th corps headquarters, to get a leave of absence for a friend, and learned that the army would move on the day following at day-break. While there, the order came to move, and among other orders was one relieving General Bartlett from command of the brigade, and assigning it to Colonel Upton. I requested the privilege of taking the order down to Upton, and did so, telling him the good and unexpected news. I knew that I would be his aid, and accordingly made arrangements to enter on my new position. The regiment was turned over to the command of Major Mather, and we left to perform new duties, my part of which were more pleasant than those of an infantry adjutant.

At day-break on the morning of the seventh of November, we commenced our march towards the Rappahannock, and about noon heard rapid and heavy firing on our left and front; in the afternoon it ceased and all was quiet again. At four P. M., we came in sight of the river, and halted in a large wood one and a half miles from the river, and rested in line of battle. By five P. M., the whole corps was concentrated. The rebels were on our side of the river in powerful force, fortified by massive redoubts and earth works. Portions of the 121st New York and 96th Pennsylvania, were detailed as skirmishers under Captain Fish of the 121st. The rebel skirmishers were along the crest of a long hill, the approach to which from our side was an open one; not a stone nor tree in the way, and the ground as even as a floor. As our line emerged from the woods, the rebels rose up and stood ready to receive us. I sat on my horse on a little knoll, with Colonel Upton, Generals Torbert and Terry and staffs, all of us watching the skirmishers; I especially, for as soon as the fire opened I was to ride rapidly back and conduct the brigade up to the place where we then were. Gradually our line approached the rebels; not a shot was fired; every moment to me seemed hours. Nearer and nearer our men advanced; still all was quiet, till at last when our line was in a few yards of them, the enemy opened fire. I waited long enough to see our men dash up the hill and disappear in the pursuit of rebels, and then started for the brigade, and in a few minutes was on my return to the front, the brigade following. We now discovered that the rebel works were very strong, and commanded the plain.

General Russel commanding the fighting men on the field determined to assault. He doubled the skirmish line by deploying the 5th Wisconsin and the 6th Maine. Those two regiments then made a most gallant charge and captured two redoubts on the right of the enemy's line, and four cannon in position. The 49th New York and the 119th Pennsylvania were then moved up to their support, encountering a severe musketry fire from the enemy, posted behind a line of rifle pits, extending to the left of these redoubts. The regiments succeeded in holding the captured works. Colonel Upton, with the 121st New York and 5th Maine, was then ordered to charge and capture these pits. The skirmishers in the mean time had kept up an incessant fire; artillery had been brought into action, and the engagement become general. About half an hour before sunset the artillery ceased firing and the musketry subsided a little.

Just as the sun was sinking, the lines of the 121st New York and 5th Maine moved forward. Upton and I rode in their front one hundred yards. As we were fairly in the open field he said to me, "In less than a minute all this artillery will open on us." At that instant a shell came whirling through the air, whose bright red fuse seemed pointed exactly for us; but it struck a short distance in our front and bounded over our heads into the midst of a band of musicians, instantly dispersing that gallant body of men. In a moment the air was full of these spiteful projectiles. Within two hundred yards of their works we halted under cover of a small hill, to form our charging columns. I was standing by my horse, writing an order on the saddle, when a shell from a battery not before known, burst near me. At first I thought I was struck, but, turning around, saw that the man waiting by my side whom I was to send with the order, was torn to pieces, his shoulder dissevered from his body. Thankful for my escape, I mounted and carried the order myself. We were ready to charge. Unslinging knapsacks, at Upton's command "charge," we dashed up the threatening line of works regardless of the storm of balls that passed through us, pressed on, and were soon at the top, and then in possession. It was quite dark, and the enemy could not see the smallness of our numbers. At this point, when our regiments had changed their front, and were about to dash on the rebel line in its flank and rear, Upton, in a voice loud enough to be heard by the enemy, cried, "The first line will lie down when fired on, as there are three others to support them." In fact we had but one line of battle; but the enemy hearing this, and thinking themselves outnumbered and overpowered when we made a vigorous charge on them, surrendered at discretion, and thereupon, with bayonet alone, our five hundred and eighty men captured fifteen hundred infantry and six colors. The rebels quietly submitted to their fate, but few escaped, and they mostly by swimming the river. One hungry or provident chap ran across the bridge, and just as he reached the other side, stopped and looked back in doubt and misery, and slapping his leg, exclaimed "there by —— I've left my flour;" but he soon concluded to starve in Dixie and ran on.

We captured every thing, men, guns, colors and camp and garrison equipage, with a loss of about one hundred men, though that was a fifth of our number. Six officers surrendered to me in person, and their swords I had at one time attached to my belt. I went to the rear to bring up the two other regiments as guards, for our prisoners outnumbered us three to one. The night was very dark and cold. I was not familiar with the ground, but was so fortunate as to find the regiments where they were left in the afternoon, and equally fortunate in conducting them back to the captured work. At two o'clock in the morning the colonel and I laid down and slept till day-light. The trophies were then collected; fifteen hundred stand of small arms, six battle flags, and quantities of other equipments. We were astonished when we saw by day-light what we had done. It was a brilliant achievement for such a handful of men to take those powerful earth works, manned by three times their number, and produced a most gratifying sensation in our army, and deep mortification in the rebel army. In his report of the affair, Colonel Upton spoke in a complimentary manner of his staff, mentioning us by name. Our adjutant general, Captain Wilson, was shot through the wrist and left us. On the afternoon of the 8th we crossed the river, and moved by wings to the front, up to Brandy station, without meeting the enemy. There we went into camp, the 2d brigade going up to the Hazel river and camping on the south side.

Presentation to General Meade.

Brandy Station was made the base of supplies, and communication opened with Washington by the Orange and Alexandria rail road. After being in camp a few days, arrangements were made to present General Meade the rebel flags captured in our late fight. Selecting fifty men from each regiment, we formed them into companies, giving each company a rebel flag, and a United States flag to fly over the rebel. In columns of companies, banners flying, and band playing, we marched out. All the troops near us turned out to see our little band, and we were cheered from our camp all the way till we reached General Meade's. At army headquarters the column was formed into line of battle, and Colonel Upton in a fitting speech presented General Meade the captured flags. The general replied in an appropriate manner, and then invited us in his tent. All the generals of note in the army were there, and after an introduction to each one, and drinking several glasses of champagne, we mounted our horses and went home.

The battle of Rappahannock station added to the former brilliant reputation of our brigade, a reputation which it maintained through the entire war.

CAMPAIGN OF MINE RUN.

The time elapsing between the affair of Rappahannock station and the 24th of March, 1863, was not marked by any event worth recording. On the morning of the 24th, the 2d corps, encamped south of Brandy station, made a movement toward the Rapidan. After marching a few miles only, it was forced to return on account of the mud caused by a heavy rain which had been falling the night previous.

The morning of the 26th broke with a cold, drizzling rain, and during the forenoon we received orders to move at one P. M. Never was a campaign commenced under less favorable circumstances. The elements were greatly against us. Our army was small, and the movement seemed to be made only to keep the great American people quiet with the question, "Why don't the army of the Potomac move?"

At two P. M., on the 26th, we drew out and moved toward Brandy station. About dark we overtook the army train; some wagons were stuck in the mud, others tipped over, and some sunk in the mud and water. To our disgust, orders were sent to our brigade to remain and help the trains out of their troubles. All night long, after the greatest exertion, we succeeded in putting the train on hard dry land. I confined my attentions during the night to Waterman's battery, and with the men under my charge, extricated his guns so many times, that he offered me the privilege of fighting one of his sections whenever I felt so disposed.

We continued the march, and at day-break on the 27th, stood on the banks of the Rapidan at Jacob's ford. The 2d corps was to cross at Chancellorsville, the 1st and 3rd at Germania, and the 5th and 6th at Jacob's ford. On the approach of our army, General Lee retired to Mine Run, six miles from the river, and there took a position of defense. The weather was growing cold, the rain did not abate, and the men were beginning to suffer. On the 28th, we moved forward through the upper part of the wilderness. Lee's skirmishers were far in front of his main lines, and therefore picket firing commenced very soon after he moved.

On the 2d of December, General French, with the 2d corps, encountered General Johnston of Early's corps. A fierce battle ensued, and at its height our brigade was sent to French's assistance. Never had I heard such dreadful rolls of musketry; the noise of the discharge of twenty thousand muskets and their reverberations through the woods was incessant and deafening; nothing but their steady whir could be distinguished, and soon the rebel batteries added their noise to that of the infantry. Our brigade was on the crest of a hill at Locust Grove under a steady stream of fire waiting for orders to charge. But the enemy retired, having lost one thousand men killed and wounded, and we seven hundred.

During the night I was riding over the field with Colonel Upton, when we met General Neil, and from him the colonel learned the disposition for the night. Upton rode rapidly off to see General Howe leaving me with General Neil. Presently the general turned to me, and said: "Orderly, when Colonel Upton returns, tell him to move his brigade in the woods, and let the men sleep." I answered, "General, I will give him the order, but I am a staff officer, and not an orderly." Thereupon the general was so profuse in his apologies, that I almost regretted that I had undeceived him as to my rank. He was called the most polite man in the army, and he always exceeded himself in his attentions to me after this mistake.

Towards morning I fell asleep on a pile of rubbish and slept till day-break, when with the remainder of the corps, we started for Mine Run. The weather was still very cold, and the troops were suffering severely, as scarcely an enlisted man in the brigade had an overcoat. On Saturday morning we reached a hill in view of Mine Run. General Lee's army was found on the crest of some hills standing in a semicircle. Between him and us, in the centre, was the run, a deep creek. All the woods in his front were felled, making an impenetrable abatis. His guns commanded every avenue of approach to every part of his lines. As soon as we saw the works the idea of assaulting them seemed preposterous, though had the order been given the attack would have been made with desperation. Upton and some general officers rode to the right of the line, and found a place where an attack seemed the most practicable, and on reporting the same to the commander-in-chief, he ordered the 5th and 6th corps to move into the dense pine woods on the right, preparatory to an assault. At a distance of about twelve hundred yards from Lee's works, we entered the woods at two o'clock on Sunday morning. Already some men had perished with the cold. Fires were not allowed, as we were to remain in the woods unknown to the enemy.

Warren, with thirty thousand men, was to attack Lee's right at eight A. M., and at nine A. M. our batteries were to open, and our two corps to charge. By day-light the affair became a matter of indifference to us, as we were just as willing and ready to be killed by iron and lead as by cold.

However, in the morning as General Lee appeared inclined to remain in his works, General Meade thought he could as well defer the battle till Monday, and thus observe the laws of Sunday.

This little sting of conscience of the general gave us twenty-four hours more to suffer the stings of this December cold, and try to freeze to death. I believe a few more men succeeded. I was afraid to sleep, and my feet and hands were aching severely. The men were thumping and jumping about to keep up circulation. Without any exaggeration I may say these three days were as cold as any we ever had in New York in the same month.

The defiant look and seemingly impregnable works of the enemy added nothing to our comfort. On Sunday all was quiet, and on Monday morning a benumbed and frozen army stood in line of battle, waiting the signal to commence the engagement. In the distance we heard the roar of Warren's artillery. The 6th corps batteries opened, and in two minutes our blood was in circulation to our hearts' (dis) content. I was sent to McCarteney's battery with an order for him to fire on a certain work. While I went through the woods the shot and shell cut down limbs and trees in front and behind me. I reached the battery out of breath, and gave the order, and waited to see the effect of the shot. He fired by battery, and turning to me said, "You better get into the woods again." The words were scarcely spoken before torrents of shells came pouring into his battery; I thought they never would stop coming, and when they did, they left us, in McCarteney's words, "sorry that we had stirred them up in the first place."

CAMPAIGN ABANDONED.

I returned to the brigade, and found it waiting for the word charge. Suddenly an aid-de-camp, followed by two more, dashed up just in time to General Sedgwick with instructions to postpone the attack. Warren had found that the rebel position on his front was too strong for him to carry. General Meade wisely determined to delay the attack, and after further examination decided to abandon the campaign and return to the north side of the Rapidan. Accordingly orders were issued for the army to retire. Colonel Upton was appointed commander of the corps pickets. The corps commenced its withdrawal at dusk. We were to remain with the pickets till three in the morning. All the staff but me went with the remainder of the brigade; I stayed with Upton. That picket business was risky. There we stayed nearly all night in sight of an army of seventy thousand men, and had only a picket line of a few hundreds for defense. At four o'clock the pickets were quietly and safely withdrawn, and marched down to Robinson's Tavern, where the army pickets were to assemble. After a discussion of rank for some time, it was decided that Upton was the ranking officer, and therefore would command the four thousand men composing the pickets of all the corps in the army. At noon we overtook the main army at the river, and as we were all across, the rebel rear guard made a slight demonstration with artillery, and then returned in their glory. Thus ended the campaign of Mine Run, a campaign which caused suffering, mortification and loss of confidence. In the course of two or three days we were back in our old camp at Brandy station.

Winter Quarters, 1863 and 1864.

We were once more on the south side of the Hazel in our old camps. Winter quarters were announced, and it behooved each one to make himself as comfortable as possible for the next five or six months. On the opposite side of the river was a large substantial house surrounded with all manner of barns and sheds. And near this house were clean pine woods and elegant grounds for camps. We tried to impress upon the colonel that it was necessary for the troops to move from their present quarters. Surgeons certified that our camp was very unhealthful, and the chaplains wanted pleasanter surroundings for their devotions. At length Upton thought as we did, and one afternoon rode up to General Sedgwick for permission to move, which he gained, and that evening we laid a pontoon bridge, and across we went — the only troops on that side of the river, and therefore completely isolated from the army. I had not slept in a house for more than a year, and many nights in that year upon the ground. So at the idea of beds and four substantial walls, I was vastly delighted. Without invitation from the lady of the house, Mrs. Major, we very politely requested her to accept us as guests for the coming winter. The brigade took possession of the woods, and its commander and staff of the house. Our staff was composed of pleasant, intelligent, witty young men, and full of life, except Captain Swift, the commissary, who was sixty-three years old, but young for his age. All were department officers. I was some of the time half-and-half, adjutant general and aid-de-camp. Our rooms were large and well fitted up. But a few yards from the house was the lovely little river, a tributary of the Rappahannock. The grounds of the house were handsomely and tastefully laid out. In fact the headquarters of Upton at Presque Isle Hall were considered to be the most aristocratic, stylish, and comfortable in the army of the Potomac. For the first few evenings we did nothing but congratulate ourselves upon our elegant quarters, and in the day time took care that the men were made comfortable. When we were somewhat accustomed to Mrs. Major's house, we concluded we would give a dinner party.

OUR DINNER.

A long list of luxuries was made out, and an agent sent to Washington to get them. General Sedgwick's staff were to be the guests, and therefore it was necessary to have enough wine. We had sufficient to float the pontoons of the 50th Engineers. The day arrived, the guests were assembled, and we sat down. The champagne had been put in a tub of water and placed out on the roof, from the hall windows, to keep cold. Skirmishing commenced with the soup, and we were comparing our present life to that of a few weeks previous, when we heard a terrific noise that sent consternation through the entertainers, if not through the guests. The case was this, while the servants were taking in the tubs, something rolled down stairs that sounded very like the crashing of champagne bottles, crash, crash followed in quick succession, every bottle appearing to be on a spree, knocking itself against every step of the stairs as it went down. The company tried that ludicrous kind of politeness of looking unconscious that any thing has occurred to annoy the host, though I saw more than one of them smile at the appearance of Hall's eyes as they started from their sockets, and of the colonel's white look about the mouth. However, in a moment our head cook entered with a smile of triumph lighting his gastronomic countenance, and holding a bottle of champagne in each hand. The alarm was occasioned by two windows falling down stairs, much to Mrs. Major's displeasure. The dinner was a success; and as the party dispersed, the adjutant general assured me that I could have a leave any time I felt disposed to apply for it.

Went Home.

There was nothing now for us to do, and I began to think the sight of Cherry Valley would not be an unpleasant one, and therefore applied for a ten days' leave. The application was returned approved. I could scarcely realize that the great pleasure of seeing my home and New York was before me. During the year which had seemed so long, I had often dreamed of that pleasure, but had not looked at the possibility of enjoying it. On the 14th of January, I rode to Brandy station to take the cars, and while waiting for the train to be made up, met my friend General Niel, who, with his usual politeness, invited me to ride in the car which was being especially prepared for him, and, of course, I accepted the invitation. My visit home was delightful, and after a few day's sojourn there and in New York, I again started for the army.

Return to the Army.

On my return to our headquarters I found at our house two of Madam Major's female friends. My introduction was more vigorous than formal. After paying my respects to our commander in his room, I went in the hall, and jumped out on the front piazza roof, and commenced hopping up and down. In a moment I heard a crash, two or three shrill screams, and then all was quiet. I went below to investigate, and found that in my enthusiasm I had knocked down all the plaster on the heads of the fair Virginians. I apologized, censured myself, was forgiven, and introduced. I had a bottle of "night blooming cereus," the perfume took, though it did not last long. Hall smelt stronger than I did, and Daniels, who was about going home to be married, excelled us both.

Presents and Punch.

For some time the idea of making General Bartlett a present had been entertained in the brigade. The money was raised, and a beautiful watch and corps badge selected as the gifts. The presentation was to take place at our headquarters, in presence of General Sedgwick and staff, and of the officers of the brigade, numbering about one hundred and fifty. Our staff held a council of provisions. Hall said that necessarily there would be a great deal of drinking, and Daniels proposed that in that case we should give the guests a great deal to drink. Swift, the commissary, remarked he had enough whisky to kill them all. Hall thought it would be a bore having forty or fifty men in the house all night sleeping under tables and hanging over bed-posts. I then proposed we should concoct a "solution of poison," strong enough to make them all tight early in the day, and by that means dispose of their society for the night. This plan was agreed to, and we set to work making the most villainous compound that man ever drank and survived. We took thirty gallons of commissary whisky with enough sugar to make it very sweet and smooth, six bottles of brandy, six bottles of gin, and weakened the whole with claret and lemons, intending when the guests arrived to retire and watch the effects, in the same way as men blasting rocks wait behind a tree for the explosion. At noon, the company began to assemble. I told my friend Madam Major not to be surprised at any thing that might occur, for there was no telling what United States officers might do on rebel ground, when their natural temperaments were a little excited — that possibly more hats and uniforms might be demolished than would suffice for a young rebel regiment. At last General Bartlett came in dazzling style; we were ready to receive him, he drank our healths in the punch, and the compliment we returned, but sparingly in point of beverage. General Sedgwick then came and took a glass of our concoction; he evidently suspected the properties of our soothing little lotion, but said nothing, and after him, others of lesser note rejoiced at our hospitality.

Chaplain Adams, of 5th Maine, made the presentation speech, and General Bartlett, with the corner of his eye a little moistened, feelingly replied, and pocketed the presents. We then commenced the part of entertainers, and offered our guests a lunch under the trees below, and punch to make them feel at ease. In a short time some were telling stories, some making speeches, and some singing songs. The most temperate grew somewhat vociferous. General Sedgwick came in the room and was assailed by numbers to listen to their exploits on the peninsula or elsewhere. Lucretia Borgia could have poisoned them all, but would have refrained, seeing how effectually her work was already done. Mrs. Major grew crazy and called on the guerillas, Moseby, and the devil, to murder us. She thought Blenker's division of Dutchmen were having a celebration. She attacked me in the hall with the words, "Adjutant, you are no gentleman to bring here those crazy Yankees."

The 2d brigade staff were not soon forgiven for this day's business. When any of our guests were afterwards asked by any of us to take a drink, they always refused, with a polite "No, I thank you."

LADIES IN THE ARMY.

By this time about twenty-five hundred ladies had arrived in the army — visiting their husbands, fathers, and brothers. Our brigade had its share, and we looked like a garrison in time of peace. As we had a fine band at our headquarters we gave several dancing parties. Hall fell in love with one young lady who did not reciprocate his passion, so he got commissioned in a colored regiment and left. Daniels's wife came to see him, and kept him out of mischief. Swift was too old to be very fascinating, and I moved among the girls generally.

General Bartlett's Ball.

In February General Bartlett gave a ball. One of his staff came over and invited us. On the appointed day ambulances were requested for the ladies. The division surgeon, a cross old M. D., refused to allow them to go. Whereupon, I rode up to General Sedgwick's, and asked him for permission to take the wagons; he told me to take all I wanted, but to look out for any *punch that tasted weak*.

The ambulances appeared, and our party started and reached the 5th corps about nine o'clock, and found a company of several hundred ladies and gentlemen dressed in the height of civil or military fashion. The male portion of the people who did not dance, generally kept out of the way of those who did. There was no respect to rank. A lieutenant dancing the galop would collide with a major general without apology. Spurs, sabres and sashes caught in dresses and coat tails; and the whole room was a scene of chaotic confusion. At one o'clock supper was announced. After supper dancing was resumed. At length, tired of dancing, about two o'clock, I thought I would go home, and accordingly my ambulance was ordered. Just as I was going out, General French was coming in, Captain Bartlett said to him, "Why, General, I thought you had gone home." The general had thought so too, but, poor man he had wandered about for an hour, and at last turned up in the same place he had started from; he had seen some headquarters, and going to them found he was in the same place where he had been all night. I reached home at peep of day, and went to sleep, thinking of ladies and Sedgwick punches. In the afternoon General Meade rode up to our headquarters and when I went out to meet him, to my surprise called me by name, and introducing me to some ladies with him, asked me to show them over our camp. I did so, and when they left I thanked fortune that there was no ball that night.

The months of February and March were occupied with rides, parties, drills and reviews. I frequently crossed the Rappahannock to visit some of my Virginian friends. One day I was at the house of a Miss Fant, and while talking with her, the 5th corps pickets were suddenly withdrawn, leaving me outside. Pickets were placed down at the ford where I had crossed, and not knowing the countersign I could not pass them. I did not intend riding by way of Rappahannock station home, a distance of twenty-two miles. Miss Fant told me the 118th Pennsylvania was on picket. In that regiment there were a great many Dutchmen, and I knew if there was one of them on guard at the ford that I could get the better of him. So I rode cautiously towards this picket, and waited till he was about two hundred yards from the river and then put my horse on a full gallop for the ford. The sentinel saw me, and gave chase, yelling halt, as if the lives of the army hung on the strength of his voice. I gained the ford, crossed and went home, and never said a word about the affair.

General Grant Appears. Banishes the Ladies.

Early in April, General Grant, having been appointed Lieutenant General, made his appearance in the army of the Potomac. Directly on his arrival an order was issued to corps commanders, that every lady in their respective corps should leave without delay. The 12th of April was fixed for the first installment of the great departure. On the morning of that sad day Captain Daniels and I rode down to see the first exodus. It required two days to remove them all. We sat on a bundle of hay till the most affecting scenes were over, and then attended to our own little business in that line. The remainder of the twenty-five hundred of our guests left on the next day, under circumstances still more heart-rending. After a proper and becoming time, we rallied and began

PREPARATIONS FOR THE CAMPAIGN.

The army was consolidated into three corps. The 2d, 5th and 6th were enlarged by the others being merged into them. Their united strength was eighty thousand men, and thirty-six batteries. With General Burnside's corps the army numbered about one hundred thousand men, nearly all of them veterans. Colonel Upton was left in command of our brigade, and General Wright of our division. As April drew to a close we looked for orders that would open the campaign. Officers and privates wrote home their last letters, rations and ammunition were issued, and on the third of

May the army of the Potomac was ready once more to measure bayonets with its enemies.

Our brigade numbered about twenty-three hundred men for duty. Our staff remained the same, except that Captain Fish was made adjutant general, and we had an extra aid in the person of Lieutenant Patterson.

Under our gallant brigade commander, we were now about to enter on the bloody fields of the Wilderness, Spottsylvania, Cold Harbor, Petersburg, and Winchester, where he won honor and distinction for himself and his soldiers.

Battles of the Wilderness.

At midnight on the 3d of May, we received orders to vacate our camps, and join the corps on the south side of the Hazel. By the morning our elegant quarters were left in solitude, and we were shivering in little tents waiting for final instructions. During the evening of the 3d I was at corps headquarters, and there learned that the corps would move at the hour of four in the morning.

My little sins during the winter came up before me, but my thoughts were turned as I saw several negroes with a coffin. They told me "Uncle Clem had gone dead, and dey was waitin' fur de preacher." I went on and met Chaplain Adams, his coat buttoned up and a big bible under his arm, looking very solemn. I remarked it was rather early in the season to go *black burying;* he deigned no reply, but looked shocked at my irreverence.

I went home, and made preparations for the morrow. At 3 A. M., on the 4th, réveille sounded; we were soon up cooking and eating, while the dark spring fog hung heavily over us. The small fires of the soldiers were just discernible. Gradually the day appeared, and the sun rose as our columns drew out in line of march. Our course was to Brandy station, and thence to Germania ford on the Rapidan, a distance of fifteen miles. The cavalry division of General Wilson had effected a crossing and laid pontoon bridges. We reached the river about six P. M., and, after crossing, moved some distance, and went into camp for the night. The other corps had crossed at other places, very much as in the Mine Run campaign. We all felt deep interest and anxiety to see how General Grant would handle the army, and how he would cope with General Lee, while the latter acted on the defensive. Upon our approach General Lee retired behind his works at Mine Run, but seeing that General Grant intended to let him stay there, he moved his forces out, and on the sixth of May struck the right of the 5th corps. We were immediately sent to the aid of that corps, and reached it, after passing through an almost impenetrable thicket.

The work of destruction had commenced; the musketry was fearful, but there was no cannonading, as artillery could not be taken through the woods. At length the firing in some degree ceased, and at sunset our lines were confronting those of Longstreet, our old enemy. Already we had lost many men without being really engaged. Colonel Carroll of the 95th was killed two minutes after he had gone to execute an order I had given him. That night was passed under a perfect shower of balls.

Friday, the sixth, commenced with heavy skirmishing. We did not know the result of the operations of the other corps, though the firing from their lines had been incessant all the night. Hancock, with the 2d corps, was on our extreme left; Warren, with the 5th, in the center; and the 6th corps on the extreme right. Between the right of the 6th corps and the river, were only a few cavalry videttes. All day we were kept down by the balls of sharpshooters. As Patterson and I were dodging behind trees, he was shot in the hand while scratching his ear. I told him it was a wonder his ear was not hit instead of his hand, for that was the larger of the two. The next day witnessed the same scenes, and the woods began to look tattered and stripped by so many balls fired into them. We wondered why all this firing was kept up without any charging, but it was kept up, and everywhere men, horses and trees were thrown about prostrate. Already our brigade had sustained a loss of two hundred men by casual shots. Saturday dawned under similar circumstances. Hancock had had a terrible battle at the Chancellorsville cross-roads, losing eight thousand men, but gallantly repulsing the enemy. About this time we heard and began to realize, that we were under a commander who "proposed to fight it out on this line if it took all summer." The tenacity of the army of the Potomac was to be more sorely tested than ever before. Thousands of men were dead and wounded, and that vast wilderness was one great cemetery and hospital for both armies. The situation was so unfamiliar to us that we did not pretend to criticise the actions of our generals, nor presume upon the result of the Wilderness fighting. Continually the rain of iron was sweeping over us, men slept on their muskets, and staff officers, with their horses saddled, were constantly on the watch. The 3d division of the corps was on the right, and in its rear were General Sedgwick's headquarters. At 5 P. M. on the 7th, there was an unusual peal of musketry in that direction, which deepened with a steady choking roll. Presently Colonel ———, of General Wright's staff, in a very demoralized condition, dashed up to our brigade, and in a terror-stricken voice yelled, "121st follow me on the double quick." Before the regimental commander could get his men in hand, they dashed off with this crazy, foolish officer. Colonel Upton and I were at the left of the brigade, and we instantly mounted our horses and dashed up to the right to see what was the matter. In five minutes the whole 3d division was rushing pell mell through our lines, completely breaking up our formation, and carrying two of our regiments by force to the rear. The balls of the enemy were crashing about us, and the 2d division line was firing with great spirit. Upton and I were separated. Portions of two regiments were with me. I was the only mounted officer there, and as I was about to give some orders on my own responsibility, General Sedgwick came rushing through the woods and told me to form a line perpendicular to the old line, and repulse the enemy coming in that direction; but no enemy came, and therefore I lost the opportunity of making myself a brigadier general. That horrible wilderness, filled with thousands of soldiers running, fighting and dying, at that time presented a scene scarcely paralleled on earth. The rebels did not press on, but were content with holding the right of our line. The first and second divisions of course held their ground, and after dark the situation was nearly the same as during the day. I knew some different formation of the corps would have to be made. Colonel Upton and I were with General Sedgwick, and the 95th and 96th Pennsylvania were with us. General Sedgwick asked me if I knew the way back to our old line. I said yes, and by his order conducted the two regiments to the remainder of the brigade. The night was extremely dark, and but for my perfect knowledge of the roads, which had been cut by our pioneers, I might have led the men into the enemy's lines. I had all the headquarters guard with me, and, I suppose, in the dark, looked like a general, at least an officer rode up to me and said, "General, can you tell me where General Sedgwick is." I knew the voice, and said, "—— he is back on this road about two hundred yards, I will send an orderly with you; but don't call me general again, if you please, for this night's performances do not throw much credit upon gentlemen of that rank." Two others presently made the same mistake, and I disabused their minds in a similar manner.

General Sedgwick determined to "refuse" the right of the corps, and orders were issued to move immediately. The movement had to be done with the greatest caution, for the rebel picket line was but a few yards from ours. At eleven o'clock, the 1st division commenced the march to the left, followed by the 2d, and then under the very noses of Longstreet's men, twenty thousand men marched out and took up a new position. We left all our dead and wounded on the field. After having fortified our new position we again commenced a flank move, and went within three miles of Spottsylvania Court House, a distance of sixteen miles from our original point. On the morning of the 9th our lines were again in position, and about six A. M., snatching a few leisure minutes, I sat down to eat something. The skirmishers in front were sending the "swifts" over us, but they were an old story, and did not excite much attention, nor disturb the actions of our men.

GENERAL SEDGWICK KILLED.

A moment after we sat down, Major Whittier, of General Sedgwick's staff, rode up, and told me that the general had been shot in the face, and was dying, and that he was going for an ambulance. I had just seen the general sitting on a rifle pit talking with his staff, and was startled and shocked to hear of the disaster to the noble hearted soldier. The sad news soon spread though the corps, and every man mourned over the great loss that had fallen on us. The general was carried to the rear, and in a short time died in the arms of his aid, Major Whittier, and was taken to his native place in Connecticut, and buried with merited honors. This loss was severely felt by the troops; the excitement of battles, and the fatigue of the campaign could never make them forget their favorite general " Uncle John."

GENERAL WRIGHT APPOINTED COMMANDER OF 6TH CORPS.

General Wright of our division was made major general, and placed in command of the corps, and

General Russell of the 3d brigade was placed in command of the division. The fighting so far had not resulted in any great advantage to us, but we were still in possession of our ground, and had not met with any great disaster and been forced to abandon the campaign, as in former times under other generals. The losses in the army were severe; our little brigade was dwindling down to very small numbers; two regiments had lost their commanding officers, together with many subordinate officers. One of our staff, Patterson, had left.

On the afternoon of the 9th we were ordered in three lines of battle to charge the rebel corps in our front. The lines were all ready, and we were sitting on our horses anxiously waiting the order to move forward, so that we might have the disagreeable duty over as soon as possible. The order seemed unwarranted, as an attack upon that portion of the rebel line was not at all likely to be successful. Suddenly a cloud of balls came in on our right flank; twenty men or more dropped about me. Upton gave the order to face to the right, and as we did so, we saw a line of the enemy advancing on our right flank. This movement of the enemy checkmated the assault, and thereby saved the lives of hundreds of our men. The enemy then opened a severe artillery fire on us, but did very little damage.

UPTON'S BRILLIANT CHARGE.

During the night we moved to the left three miles, and made extensive earthworks. Towards noon the heretofore steady firing in our front ceased, and we concluded to sleep a little. As we were nearly asleep, a staff officer rode up, saying that "General Wright would like to see Colonel Upton." There was no use in sleeping now, for we knew we would have fighting soon if Upton had any thing to say about it. After a while I did fall asleep, and was awakened by the voice of the colonel: "Wake up, adjutant, and mount your horse." I jumped up and saw the Vermont brigade and the 9th Pennsylvania, 121st New York and 119th Pennsylvania marching past without knapsacks. I did not ask any questions, for these twelve regiments, the flower of the 6th corps, were in their costume to "charge," and I soon found out that we were to make one of the most desperate assaults of the war. Upton told me he had been selected to take command of the regiments, mass them in the woods two hundred yards from the rebel line, and, upon the given signal, to charge and break their line. The ground between the lines was as even as a floor, and so well commanded by the artillery and infantry of the enemy, that nearly every shot would have great effect. We were to break the line, turn to the right, and clear a space in the enemy's works equal to the front of one of our divisions. General Mott, of the 2d corps, if we were successful, was to charge on our left, and protect our rear and flank. At six P. M., the batteries ceased firing, and as they did so, the clear voice of Upton rang out, "Attention! Forward!" when all the lines rose up, the three first to advance, the fourth to move to the edge of the woods, and cover the retreat if there should be any. Like one man, that immense mass of thousands of men rose up, and instantly were met by a severe and staggering fire, but passed or rushed over the works, drove the gunners from their guns, and turned the battery on the enemy. We then wheeled to the right, and carried every thing before us.

Nothing was able to stand that torrent of the picked men of the 6th corps so bravely led. Twelve hundred prisoners surrendered, and were sent to the rear. We were performing our portion of the work with magnificent success, when suddenly every kind of missile came crashing into us. We were attacked by the remainder of Ewell's corps, and by their superior numbers were completely carried back. General Mott's division had refused to charge, and, therefore, our charge at first so successful, was turned into a repulse, and we had to retreat, leaving twelve hundred of our men on the field.

We retired to our former position. Of the eight hundred men in our brigade, four hundred and two were killed and wounded in this charge. The woods were full of these unfortunate creatures, and sounded all night with their cries and groans. The charge would have been a brilliant success had not its supports entirely failed.

The incessant roar of battle for so many days had begun to affect the nerves and strength of the men. Peal after peal of thousands of muskets would startle the whole army from a deep and greatly needed sleep; for six days not fifteen minutes had elapsed that we did not hear the rattle, and see the effects of these infernal engines of war. Grant was plainly demonstrating to the army of the Potomac that it must make this the last campaign and finish the rebellion.

The 12th of May—Spottsylvania Court House.

The 12th of May, 1864, will ever be remembered by the 6th and 2d corps as the date of one of the most desperate and bloody struggles, and one of the most brilliant victories of the war. And our gallant colonel, too, will remember the day, for at that time by his personal exertions, daring and skill, he won for himself lasting honor, and the merited rank of brigadier general, the order conferring on him that rank declared it to be "for meritorious and gallant conduct during the battles of the Wilderness, and for the battle at Spottsylvania Court House, on the 12th of May, 1864."

At day-break on the 12th, Hancock assaulted the enemy, taking him completely by surprise, capturing one entire division with its commander, General Johnston, and eighteen pieces of artillery, and obtaining possession of the key of his works. Our brigade was ordered to move forward to assist the 2d corps. The 121st and 96th were in front advancing into a break in the 2d corps, and were met with a heavy fire which they returned, and in five minutes were hotly engaged. The other two regiments were ordered up, and they opened fire. Less than forty yards from us were the rebels in very strong force, pouring the most destructive fire into us. Between the two lines was a rifle pit which each side was contending for, but which neither could get; and there twenty thousand men were sending balls into the unprotected breasts of their opponents. It seemed impossible that troops could stand so severe a fire. I called up two orderlies to give them an order, and while speaking to them both their horses were hit, and I had to carry it myself. There was one steady stream of iron and lead from the whole of A. P. Hill's corps. I sat on my horse thinking that if I lived fifteen minutes I would do better than I could hope for. At 9 A. M., the rain began to fall and came down in torrents, the mud was over a foot deep, and the men in ranks eight or ten deep, slipped and stood firing at will. Upton and his staff were busy in keeping the men in position; openings would occur, made by volleys of balls, and would be instantly closed by the supply of other men. The rebels tried to form columns to charge us, but our dreadful fire broke up their formation before they were ready. We tried the same thing, and were equally unsuccessful. Already there were heaps of our dead lying about and impeding our operations. Our troops got gunpowder crazy, and standing up in the most exposed position, would fire with deliberate aim. The rebels still held their ground, and we ours, fighting behind breastworks made by the dead of both armies.

Toward noon Upton told me to ride back, and get a section of artillery to put in position where we were. I went and asked a captain of artillery for two pieces, and he sent them up, remarking that he never expected to see them again. Back I went with the guns, and they were put in position, and fired just one round of canister, when every man at the guns was killed or wounded.

A Rebel Trick Detected.

Early in the afternoon the rebels displayed a white flag, in the midst of about eighty men, who were deployed as skirmishers, and who advanced towards us apparently with the intention of surrendering. We were about ordering our men to cease firing, when we saw a line in rear with muskets trailed that did not look much like a surrender; whereupon a strong fire was opened on the eighty men, killing a good many, and taking the rest prisoners. From them we learned that under cover of that white flag, the rebels were to charge our position; but they decidedly got the worst of the operation, as it turned out.

INCREASED CARNAGE.

The battle had now raged into one of fierce determination; the best troops of each army were opposed, and it seemed that nothing but the death of all would decide the affair. Horses were killed, and their bodies were so cut up that there was not a bone of them left as large as a finger; men were so mutilated that they could not be recognized by their comrades. Captain Fish, our adjutant general, was killed. We were standing in mud up to our knees, wet through, and head, eyes and ears aching from the effects of the ordeal we were passing through. Our men had fired on an average three hundred rounds of cartridges each. Every thing for a mile in our rear was greatly cut up. I remember there was one tree just in front, twenty-two inches in diameter, through which a shell had passed in the morning, and before night it was cut down and in fine splinters by musket balls.

At four P. M., after ten hours of this carnage, we were relieved, and fresh troops took our place. Three hundred would not cover the loss in our brigade, a dreadful one for the numbers engaged. Another of our staff had gone, leaving Sanbourn and I next to be called for. Upton's horse was killed, but mine and myself were untouched. We moved down into the woods, and the men were permitted to lie down and sleep. During the remainder of the afternoon, and until three o'clock the next day, the firing was steady, and unbroken, when the rebels gave way, leaving us in possession of one of the bloodiest battle fields ever known.

The Bloody Angle.

On the morning of the 13th, we returned to the "bloody angle" as our previous day's battle ground had been called, and there saw a sight that is indescribable. On one side of the pits were hundreds of our dead piled on each other, bodies perfectly powdered, and bones cut up as fine as dust. On the rebel side, in a space of less than an acre, lay in piles the disfigured bodies of four hundred and fifty of our enemies. Woods in the rear, several acres in extent, were cut down by shot, shell and bullets. Not a vestige of the rebel camps was left; nothing had escaped the terribleness of our fire. The stubbornness evinced by both armies that day plainly showed why the war lasted as long as it did, and taught us that nothing but a total route and capture of Lee's army would ever give peace.

In the night of the 13th we were ordered to follow the 5th corps to Spottsylvania Court House. The night was very dark, windy and rainy. Our brigade was to lead the corps, so I was sent ahead to a certain cross roads to wait there until the rear of the 5th corps was passing, and then let Upton know. I went there, dismounted, and sat down under a tree, watching the troops. I was feeling very blue, tired and worn out, sick of seeing dead and wounded. The small fires on the road side threw a dim light on the passing soldiers, but enough for me to see how tired and haggard each man looked. It was a sad time to me. At length the rear guard passed, and I sent an orderly to the general, as I always called Upton after the 12th. In a few minutes the long line of our men was visible, and just as the last of the 5th corps passed, we moved into the road, and after several hours of slipping and sliding in the mud reached Spottsylvania Court House, at day-break on the 14th.

Battle of Bleak Hill. 14th of May.

General Eustace, commanding the 3d brigade, was temporarily in command of the division, and was ordered by General Meade to send a brigade to occupy a place called "Bleak Hill," until he could concentrate the army, and form the line of battle near the hill. General Eustace sent our brigade, with a reinforcement of two New Jersey regiments. We numbered with them, nearly twelve hundred men. On the top of the hill was a house; putting a look-out on the top, and arranging our lines, we entered the house. This was the second time since the campaign opened that I took off my boots; my feet were raw, my boots had become part of me. As this seemed a good opportunity, we thought we would improve the time and have a rest, but scarcely were we lain down when the look-out called that there were rebel skirmishers on our right and front, one mile off. In front of the house was a plain a few hundred rods wide, and on the other side a large wood. General Upton thought he would send skirmishers to the edge of the wood and not be surprised by any rebels. Just as we were ready, Generals Meade and Wright rode up, and Upton told them his intention, and moved forward. As we got nearly to the woods we were welcomed by a very stiff infantry fire, much to our surprise, and Generals Meade and Wright turned their horses' heads, and in a hurried manner went to the rear. I looked after them, and wished myself a major general. We soon met too many men for our skirmishers, and Upton told me to bring up the 5th Maine, and I started for them. The dust flew up as the balls plowed in it. The plain was fairly alive with balls. I brought up the regiment, under a galling fire, just in time to see the skirmish line slowly retiring on our main line. We collected our little force in rear of our works, and waited for the attack which was soon made. One line of battle came out of the woods, followed by another, and another, until four lines were in plain sight, each one greater in number than all our force. Presently a light eight gun battery came out and opened with shell and canister. Our troops commenced firing, and the rebels advanced with flying colors at a charge of bayonets.

An Escape.

Seeing a break in our lines, I galloped off to learn the cause, and found that a certain regiment had disappeared. I was returning to the general with the intelligence, when I saw a large number of rebels on the hill where I had just left him. I thought it singular that we had captured so many prisoners in so brief a time. As I approached them, I noticed that the prisoners had guns in their hands, and did not see any of our own men among them. But by the time I was within fifty yards of them I apprehended the fact, that in my absence from one part of the line, it had been broken, and before I could get to another, it too had gone, leaving me in an independent situation. These *prisoners* were a line of battle, and discovered me about the time I discovered them. I turned my horse's head toward the 5th corps, as my way to the rear direct was cut off, and, as I turned, I sincerely think there were one hundred shots fired at me. My ears were fairly singed by the close firing. The fleetness of my horse and the inaccuracy of the rebel aim saved me from capture or death. After a long ride I came out in the 5th corps, and soon discovered my brigade, and found out that I had been given up as lost.

The whole army were on hills in rear, and saw the battle, though it occurred so suddenly that they could not assist us. The brigade had been overpowered, and our retreat was justifiable. General Lee in his report of the affair admits a loss of one hundred and sixty-one, while ours was ninety-eight killed and wounded. I was on the line all the time the firing was going on, but in my capacity of aid-de-camp, I had to ride to all points necessary to be attended to, and just as I left one part that broke, and before reaching the other that broke likewise, leaving me out entirely. The brigade was very much shattered, but by night was collected, and, moving in rear of the division, was permitted to sleep. During the night the rebels evacuated the hill, and the division moved up without opposition. General Lee had learned all he wanted to know, and therefore ordered his troops to retire.

On the morning of the 15th we moved up on the hill and joined the division. The day was passed very quietly, an exception to the two previous weeks. Until this day I had no idea of our losses. The division was beginning to look greatly altered, having their men as aids, as colonels, and as other officers. The new aids-de-camp were not of the best material, and therefore the old circle of staff officers was rather limited. Our brigade was dreadfully decimated. We had lost thirteen hundred men and forty officers, among the latter many of my best associates. Lieutenant Gordon, of the 95th was appointed aid with me, and I began to think whether I would outlast him. After remaining on Bleak hill for a day or two, we were ordered to be in readiness to charge with the 2d corps, and moved to the right of the army line for that purpose; but for some unknown reason we did not make the charge, and returned to our former position on the hill.

On the 17th, the 2d Connecticut heavy artillery joined the corps, and General Wright assigned the regiment to our brigade. This immense regiment numbered nineteen hundred men for duty, commanded by Colonel Kellogg, an able officer. With this reinforcement our strength was twenty-four hundred men, at that time a very respectable brigade. One night, just as we were lying down to sleep, the sound of distant rattle of musketry came to our ears, and grew into a prolonged roar. We were puzzled to find out the direction it came from. The noise was not from the right quarter to satisfy us that it was altogether legitimate fighting; it was too much to our right and rear to make us feel easy. At 11 P. M., a staff officer rode up to our headquarters with orders for us to accompany the division where the firing was. In a few minutes the brigade was under arms and on the march. As we moved the firing grew more and more distinct until day-break, when it ceased. Upon our reaching the spot, we found that Ewell's corps had made a forced march of twenty-five miles to get in our rear, and there attack us, and at the same time to capture our wagon train, which was "parked" in that vicinity. But the gallantry of General Tyler's division of heavy artillery steadily repulsed the enemy after a night's desperate fighting. As I rode over the field I was grateful that General Tyler had succeeded without our assistance. The dead and wounded in the woods, and articles of every description pertaining to soldiers strewn about, plainly showed how desperate the conflict had been.

March to the Pamunkey.

The time from the 18th to the 20th was passed in marching and skirmishing until we reached a place twenty-five miles from the Pamunkey river. After a few hours rest we resumed our course, and made a forced march of twenty-five miles, reaching the river in the afternoon of the 27th, and crossing in rear of Sheridan's cavalry encamped on the banks of the river. One day was taken to recuperate the corps, and then we made a movement forward, and strongly entrenched ourselves. The other corps were performing their respective duties in this one of the flank movements of General Grant. On the 30th, towards evening, the division was ordered on the road to Hanover Court House, and we reached the Court House after considerable skirmishing; and then after going twenty-four hours deprived of food, we returned without, to our knowledge, accomplishing any thing whatever. On our return Mr. Mosby was very polite in his way. Our cook was on the road to meet us with a cold dinner, when this ranger met him, and relieved him of dinner and every thing else. We rejoined the corps on the 1st, and moved within fourteen miles of Richmond. We then formed lines of defense, and remained all night in line of battle, expecting to attack the enemy at ten A. M. in the morning of the 1st of June; but as the rebel works were too strong, an assault was not deemed practicable, and therefore General Wright ordered the position to be abandoned. This was done upon the representation of Generals Upton and Russell.

Battle of Cold Harbor.

On the 1st of June, the 6th corps moved to Cold Harbor, eight miles from Richmond, and there found the enemy under Beauregard strongly entrenched. In front of their works, was a plain of nearly seven hundred yards in width, over which their guns had full sway. As soon as the rebel position was fully known, the decision was made to charge them. The whole corps was formed in three lines of battle; our brigade was put in the first line, the 18th corps from the peninsula, General Smith, was on the right, and the rest of the army was acting partially on the defensive; our batteries were brought on the plain, and opened on the rebel works with a scathing fire; the enemy replied with their usual vigor, and again there were stirring times. The situation was as dubious a one as I ever saw: to charge across a plain exposed to the fire of twenty thousand rifles, and any number of batteries, seemed almost madness. We were to charge at six o'clock, and the signal was to be the cessation of the firing of our batteries. I was standing talking with Gordon, when a fragment of a shell, that burst very close to us, struck him on the shoulder; he jumped up and I caught him. Most wonderfully the shell had not injured him, and he remained with us. At six o'clock our guns ceased firing, and we advanced. The enemy opened fire instantly, and our men at a "charge bayonets," did as they had many times before done, rushed across the field up to the muzzles of the rebel guns, and carried their works, driving the rebels back to their second line, two hundred and fifty yards in the rear of the first. But there they rallied, and successfully held their position. During the night the enemy made frequent attempts to drive us out of the captured work, but each time were bloodily repulsed.

On the morning of the 2d, we discovered our true situation. During the charge on the previous day we lost four hundred and eighty men out of our brigade. Colonel Kellogg of the 2d artillery was killed; the conduct of that regiment in this, its first battle, was splendid, and did great credit to their state. All day there was steady firing, and the two armies, being within two hundred and fifty yards of each other; the result of the firing was most deadly; each man had a hole or tree for protection. About noon the general rode off somewhere, and Captain Sanborn went with him. Gordon was also away, and I was alone at headquarters. An orderly came to me with an order from General Wright, that the division would charge at five P. M. on that day. I read the order with an amazement. What could General Wright mean by murdering our men in that manner? Between our line and that of the rebels was an impassable swamp, an attempt to cross which had never entered our minds. General Wright evidently had not been to the front lately, and was ignorant of the situation of the land. I despatched an orderly with a note to General Upton, and then mounted my horse, and rode to division headquarters, and asked General Russell if he knew the nature of the ground in our brigade front. He said yes, and was going to General Wright and have the order countermanded. By great urging the corps commander was induced to come to the front, long enough to see the ground; and when he saw eighty dead, black, bloated bodies of the 2d Connecticut lying about he concluded to defer the assault until four A. M. of the next day. Though General Wright had countermanded the order he did not improve on it much, by only deferring it until the next morning. It certainly seemed pleasanter to be killed in a delightful afternoon, than on a dark morning before breakfast. At midnight, however, we received an order again countermanding the assault.

The day was passed in continual firing. We were losing a great many men by chance shots, and the effect was demoralizing on the troops. Every one, private and officer, laid low, regardless of appearances. At seven o'clock P. M., on the 4th, the whole rebel line in our front rose up in their pits, and commenced a most furious fire. Our men returned this fusilade, and for half an hour there was nothing to be heard but the steady roll of musketry, and *zip* of the balls as they flew over our heads. After the affair was over I could not learn of a single man on our side that was injured, and I think the rebels fared equally as well. The two following days and nights were passed in the same way. The other corps in the meantime having some desperate battles which resulted in our favor.

Our postmaster was a man who found by sad experience at the battle of Bull Run, that fighting was not his forte, and therefore applied for and received the appointment of postmaster in our brigade. One night at Cold Harbor, while taking the letters out of the bag, he came across one for me, and when in the act of handing it to me, about five thousand balls and shells came crashing through the trees, he, without ceremony, turned and left, taking my letter with him, and leaving me his hat, which, in his hurry to stand from under, jumped off his head, and was not claimed by him for forty-eight hours afterward.

BURYING THE DEAD.

On the 7th, Generals Grant and Lee agreed to a cessation of hostilities for two hours, for the purpose of burying the dead, lying between the lines. There were several hundred bodies which had been exposed to the hot sun for six days, and were in such a state of decomposition, that both sides suffered greatly from the odor arising from them. As the burial parties were engaged in this sad duty, both armies stood on their respective works, and commenced shaking their blankets, the first opportunity they had had for a week to perform any job of this kind, for rebel balls and our balls had kept both sides down rather low. Clouds of dust arose from the plain by this needed operation of putting things in order. Here were two hostile armies within two hundred yards of each other, under certain laws of war, just as harmless as lambs, and could be, in one moment, under other rules, destructive as devils. At six, precisely, a battery thundered forth a signal for hostilities to be resumed. Like magic the two corps disappeared behind their works, and renewed the scathing fire.

Sneaking Up and Grubbing Under.

The daring of some of the men is worthy of mention, and especially of one Yankee in the 2d Connecticut, who, under cover of darkness, crawled up to the rebel pit, and pulled off the streamer of a battle flag, and returned in safety with his trophy. The colonel of the regiment was in our tent as the man went past, and asked him how he got it, and he expressed himself as follows: "I seed this thing hanging over the reb's pit, so I kind o' sneaked up, grubbed under and snatched it baldheaded, and dug for home." The colonel, in presence of Upton, thinking to be very military, said to the venturesome fellow with a frown, d—n it sir, say advance, say advance, not *sneak*. The general thought the man's description was in keeping with his mode of capture.

Sickness and Kindness.

Exposure, hardships and the fire I had been subjected to, were having a detrimental effect upon me, and bringing me down to light marching order, though fortunately I never grew dispirited. I forced up all my hilarious feelings, and drove off fear, and for a long time kept up without showing any signs of succumbing. On the night of the 10th of June, the corps was ordered to cross the Chickahominy, by making a long detour to the right and rear. That night I was unable to sit on my horse, and the general ordered up an ambulance for me, and at dark we withdrew to make another flank attack. The army left Cold Harbor with fifteen thousand men less than when it went there. At day-break we were a few miles from the James river, and there formed line of battle, and built fortifications. Here we remained until Wednesday the 15th, and then moved down to Wilcox landing. There we received orders to join General Butler at Bermuda Hundreds, and at dark our headquarters moved on board the steamer Thomas Powell, which I had often seen on the Hudson. That was the first refreshing night we had passed since the 4th of May, and was improved by all in soundly sleeping. At daylight the rough réveille awoke us, and the debarkation commenced. When all the troops were on land the line of march was begun for Point of Rocks, where we remained all day. I had done all in my power to combat the insidious disease that was rapidly gaining a firm hold upon me, but in vain, to a great extent, and therefore was beginning to feel greatly reduced in strength, and unable to continue the arduous duties of a staff officer in this terrible campaign. One night while at Point of Rocks, as we were all sleeping under the trees, an order came for the brigade to move out a short distance, and in connection with General Ames charge the enemy at twelve o'clock. The order came from General Butler, and was quickly obeyed. All the staff was called up but me. I was not awakened. Silently the general covered me with his robe, and he and his staff rode off on their fearful errand, leaving one man with me as a guard while I slept. A little after midnight I awoke, and found myself a Robinson Crusoe style of soldier, and saw the guard sitting on a stump polishing "Old Jane" as he called his musket.

My destitution of companions was explained by him. Never shall I forget the kindness of General Upton to me, on that and many other occasions. At day-break the brigade returned after a night passed standing, waiting for the order to charge; but in its stead came one from the lieutenant general, countermanding the order, and returning all the troops to their camp.

In a few days we left Point of Rocks and went to Petersburgh, and were in severe skirmishing all one day until late at night. For several days we were under heavy shell firing, and suffered to a great extent. I was now in a state too weak to be of further use on the staff. The army had reached its destination, and would probably remain at Petersburgh until the surrender of the city, and therefore would have no further very active staff duty. Dr. Kelley, the surgeon of the division, after an examination, certified, that I must leave the army for a time, or the consequences would either be fatal, or lead to evil results for life; whereupon General Wright gave me an order to report to Washington for medical treatment. Reluctantly I bid my friends good-bye, and for a few minutes my spirits were never more depressed than in being separated from my old associates in danger. After a ride in an ambulance of fifteen miles over a rough road with heat at 99°, I reached the army train on the banks of the James, and there stopped to remain all night, with my friend Captain Daniels, who received me with open arms. The warmth of his reception and the cool quiet place his tent was in, made me hope I would recover there; but the feeling soon wore off, and I was anxious to be in Washington. I went to City Point and there took the steamer for Washington. As we steamed up the river, I sat on deck thinking how fortunate I was to be one of the survivors of the old army of the Potomac, that had left tens of thousands of its soldiers between the Rapidan and the James. After remaining a few hours at Fortress Monroe, I sailed to Washington, and arrived there on the 22d, at noon, totally used up.

Taking a carriage I drove to Willard's, and immediately went to bed.

A RED HEADED SURGEON.

A red headed army surgeon came to see me, and, after much expostulation and entreaty on my part, permitted me to remain in the hotel, instead of going to some dirty hospital. He left powders and pills, and foolishly I took them all, ate just as I was directed, and at the end of five days was nearer dying than ever before. A contract surgeon's conscience is as bare as a rebel treasury shelf, and on the sixth day the doctor told me I must go to Annapolis and stay there until I got well. I listened to the little man in amazement. Would the United States government force an officer living at a hotel at his own expense, and trying to cure himself of a disease contracted in the line of his duty, to go to a hospital, a depot of pestilence? I remonstrated with my medical friend: I told him I could get well in two weeks if left where I was; but all in vain, till finally I requested him to give me convalescent papers, and I would return to my command, where at least I would find friends. This he was induced to do, and accordingly on the

28th of June I was on the Potomac, on the way back to the corps. As the ambulance stopped in front of our headquarters every one was surprised to see me, though not many questions were asked, for my sunken cheeks told their own story. However, I informed them that I returned at my own request.

That night the corps was ordered to Reams station, to assist the cavalry of General Wilson out of a predicament they had fallen into. Once more in the saddle, surrounded by old friends, and helped by a little "Dutch courage," I had strength enough to last till we returned, but then had a speedy and severe relapse.

Movement Threatening Washington.

General Lee had sent Early north to make a demonstration on Washington. Two of the three divisions of our corps, the second and third, had followed to intercept him, and at last our division, the first, was ordered direct to Washington. We found the people of the city in great consternation, but they breathed freer and deeper, when the veterans of our division marched across Pennsylvania avenue, up the Seventh street road to Fort

Stevens. Early, with thirty thousand men, as was supposed, was within a few hundred yards of the defenses of the city. Our 1st and 2d division engaged and drove back his skirmish line, and he, well aware of the character of the foe before him, wisely retreated during the night, and in the morning we followed for two days without overtaking him.

My strength and health now wholly failed, and on a second order from General Wright, I went to Washington, and thence to New York. Arriving there in the dog days, I found every one of my friends out of town, so I took the boat on the Hudson, and the next forenoon was in my old home.

Cherry Valley in Summer.

Cherry Valley was delightful. The season was unusually gay and pleasant. The town was full of elegant and fashionable people; and rides, drives, balls, parties, morning and evening concerts, picnics, dinner parties and lake parties were incessant and charming. I was every moment impressed by the immense contrast afforded by such a state of society as this, and by the lovely and thrifty country around, to the war stricken and beggarly towns and country of Virginia, which had been so familiar to my eyes. When I remembered some of the F. F. V.'s whom I had seen at their homes, almost in rags, and then looked at the photographic views of groups of some of our F. F.'s taken that summer, showing what kind of *rags* they were clothed in, the boasted superiority of the chivalric races of the South, was far from being apparent to my youthful understanding. There were no traces of war here, save in the patriotic enthusiasm of the people; and when I remembered, in contrast, the ruin, desolation, and woe, which I had everywhere seen on the sacred soil of the South, I realized how the guilty were being punished, how severely the devil was treating his own.

General Upton Wounded, and Change of Plans.

I staid at home part of the month of July, and the whole of August, and having greatly improved in health, was on the point of starting for the army, and had gone to New York on my way thither, when I heard of the battle of Winchester, won through the skill and heroism of General

Upton, and learned from him that he was wounded, and that he would be at his home in Batavia, in a few weeks. He wrote that he was entitled to an aid while on leave, and that I might join him when and where I pleased.

The battle of Winchester was the only one the 6th corps had been engaged for two years, in which I had not been a participator, and I regretted that I was not there to witness the conduct of General Upton, who on that day won praise and unsolicited promotion, soon after the battle receiving the appointment of brevet major general. When he was at his home, I went to Batavia, and after making a short visit there, we went to Niagara Falls, and then I returned home. Early in November the general made me a short visit at Cherry Valley, and then went to New York. I followed him in a day or two, and from there we went to Washington. Upon application to the war department, orders were given him to report to Major General James Wilson, commanding "Cavalry of the military division of the Mississippi," at Nashville, Tennessee, for the purpose of taking command of one of the divisions of that corps. The order mentioned that he would report as soon as his wound would enable him to resume active duty. We went up the Shenandoah valley to see our old friends, and bid them good-bye; going first to Harper's Ferry, and thence to the encampment of the 6th corps. The corps during the summer and fall campaigns had lost nineteen thousand men, and was to me greatly changed in every aspect. After remaining in the valley a few days, and saying farewell to our friends in the army of the Potomac, we went to Winchester, intending to start from there on our journey westward. But the general's wound had again broken open, and was proving so troublesome that he was unable immediately to resume duty, and therefore we concluded to make a short visit to some of our old army friends in the coal regions of Pennsylvania. After inspecting the wonders of those parts, we separated, with the arrangement that I was to join him in Nashville, in ten days. I visited Cherry Valley for a few days, and then went directly west, and on my way received a telegram to report at Louisville, and not at Nashville.

Perils on the way to Louisville.

From Rochester to Cleveland I had the care of a young lady to the latter place, and though we both fell asleep, neither of us complained of the tedium of the trip. Upon our arrival at Cleveland the young lady's friends met her, and I stepped on the night train for Cincinnati.

After jolting all night, we stopped at Xenia, a few miles from Cincinnati, and immediately the car that I was in was filled with school girls on their way home. The car had but few people in it, and was forthwith flooded with these bread and butter misses. In less than two minutes I was surrounded, and the only part of me visible was my hat, sticking above all this crinoline. I was the only representative of the male persuasion in the cars, and my natural modesty and diffidence had a sore test. The seat in front of me was turned over facing me, and two girls took possession of that, and another sat down in my seat by my side. Band boxes, hat boxes and bonnets were pitched about, perfectly regardless of consequences. I wished I had stayed in the army of the Potomac, or had come the day before or after. They only went a few miles, and, bidding me good morning, left. I managed to collect my faculties before we reached Cincinnati. I remained over Sunday in that city, and then went to Louisville, and stopped at the Galt House.

AT LOUISVILLE, KENTUCKY.

I inquired for the general at the office of the hotel, and learned that he had gone to Memphis, to be absent ten days. I therefore had nothing to do but find amusement for the next week, and contained myself with as much patience as possible. I then learned from him that our division was to be the 4th, and be organized in Louisville, and that our headquarters would be at the Galt House, all which was very satisfactory to me.

PROMOTION. VISIT NASHVILLE.

In January 1865, I received a commission as captain as a New Year's present. The general wrote to the secretary of war, telling that honorable personage of my operations during the war, and requested permission for me to be mustered as captain, and remain on duty with him as aid-de-camp. In reply, permission was given. I had but little to do while at Louisville for a while. Most of our troops had not yet arrived, and until they came there would not be any very urgent business. One night Upton told me that he desired me to go to Nashville the next day, to consult the adjutant general of the cavalry on business connected with the division. The next morning at day-break, I went to the Nashville depot, and entered the cars and seated myself. I had heard a great deal of the noted guerillas Sue Mundy, Champ Ferguson, Dick Taylor and the like, and of their barbarities on this road, and thought that now I had a good chance of meeting these gentlemen of the pad, though I did not hanker for the pleasure. The train moved out, and we went very well, so well, that the energetic engineer gained twenty minutes in forty miles. When we reached Elizabethtown, forty-two miles from Louisville, we were just twenty minutes ahead of time. This probably saved our lives; as we learned by telegram on reaching Bowling Green on the Tennessee line, that Dick Taylor entered Elizabethtown, just as our train was moving out, intending to capture the train and its inmates. As a general thing this bloody villain killed all the United States soldiers, who were unfortunate enough to fall in his hands. He was on time and our train ahead, I think for the first and last time.

I reached Nashville at 9 P. M. The first thing I saw was a street fight. I did not mix in, but went direct to corps head quarters and transacted my business that night, and was ready to leave the city at day-break the next day. I declined an invitation from Colonel Beaumont, to stay all night with him, and returned to the St. Cloud which although the best hotel in the city, was a very dirty, ill kept house. At day-break I was up and returned to Louisville, without further trouble, reaching my hotel late at night, and reported my business to the general.

Burning of the Galt House.

As I was much fatigued on the night of my return from Nashville, I retired soon after I reached the hotel. About one o'clock at night, I was awakened by a singular noise, and perceived that the room was flooded with a bright light, and full of smoke. I sprang from bed, and looked out of the window, which opened on the court, and then discovered that the whole side of the hotel was in flames. My first thought was for the general who was unable to help himself, on account of his wound. I therefore rushed down to his room, and saw that his servant had taken care of him. I ran back to my room, but found that, from the smoke and heat, I could not stay there long enough to pack up any thing, and left, thankful that I was able to escape with my life. As I went out of my door I saw that the hall was on fire, and then made quick time for the lower part of the house. When I reached the lower hall, what a sight met my eyes! Knowing every thing I had was burned, I determined to assist others as much as possible, and especially the weaker sex. There were more than four hundred and fifty guests in the house, and over half females. When the fire broke out the ladies did not stop for appearances; forms in white flitted about; all manner of millinery work was lavishly displayed; figures were seen in garments well adapted for flying; a ballet dancer would have considered herself rich in costume compared with that demoralized crowd of tea drinkers. Down stairs pell mell, went men, women and children, treading and falling over each other, till at last they all reached the first floor, and escaped the flames; all but two men who lost their lives, the hall in front of their rooms being consumed before they were aroused. The hotel was soon untenable in every part, and the suffocating and stifling coal smoke rushed so quickly through the halls, that but little could be saved even in those quarters most remote from the fire.

This was the second time, since I had been in

the army, that I had lost every article of clothing save what was on my back. The general and I forthwith went to the Louisville hotel, and by morning were comfortably settled. The next day I drew for money, and repaired damages.

After remaining in Louisville about six weeks, our division was organized and ready for the field. General Allen, chief quartermaster, had steamers ready to take us to Eastport, Mississippi, where the corps was rendezvoused. A few days before we left, General Sweeny (of late Fenian fame) gave a dinner to which General Upton and I were invited. There were several generals present, and one colonel old enough to be a general. I was a minor, but once in a while put in my opinion, and when I did not, took a drink. After a stupid dinner for me, we left the table for other engagements.

Organization and Destination of the Expedition.

On the 3d of February, 1865, the 4th division headquarters moved on board the United States steamer Tarascon, to sail down the Ohio and up the Tennessee rivers to Eastport, Mississippi. The division had preceded us several days. The distance to our point of destination was about nine hundred miles, which, after eight days of plowing through ice, and being fired at by guerillas, we reached in safety, and moved our division to Gravelly Springs, on the other side of the river in Alabama. Our headquarters were established, and once more we were back in our old familiar life. Our staff, with one humble exception, was composed of good soldiers, men of ability, intelligence and good humor. They were gentlemen, and bound together by ties of mutual respect and friendship. It was constituted as follows, twelve in number: Brevet Major James Latta, assistant adjutant general; Captain Francis W. Morse, aid-de-camp; Captain Thomas Gilpin, aid-de-camp; Major Robert Williams, assistant inspector general; Captain James Simpson, assistant quartermaster; Doctor D. W. Green, surgeon-in-chief; Captain De Grasse, provost marshal; Captain Thomas Brown, assistant commissary of subsistence; Lieutenant Leech, ordnance officer; Lieutenant Keck, ambulance officer; Captain Rogers, chief of escort.

Major Latta was from Philadelphia, and a better companion in hardship or pleasure could not be found. Gilpin, my associate aid, was the very man I wanted, full of wit, quick and energetic. I doubt if twelve men could be collected who suited each other better. General Upton was our model of a soldier; few men equaled him in talent and bravery, and fewer still in kindness and softness of disposition and manner.

The whole cavalry corps, under command of Major General Wilson, numbered about sixty thousand men. It was divided into seven divisions, of which three divisions, the 1st, 2d and 4th, were in this expedition, and were accompanied by General Wilson in person. The 1st division was commanded by Brigadier General Edward McCook, the 2d by Brigadier General Eli Long, and the 4th by Brevet Major General Emory Upton. These three divisions numbered about eighteen thousand men for duty. Our division, the fourth, contained five thousand men for duty, and one battery; it was divided into two brigades, the first commanded by Brigadier General Winslow, and the second by Brigadier General Alexander; and the battery was commanded by Lieutenant Rodney of the 4th U. S. artillery. Brevet Major General Wilson, the commander of the corps, and of this expedition, was a young man in whom Lieutenant General Grant deservedly reposed great confidence.

We were in the wilds of Alabama; immense forests stretched out on all sides, and it was a striking spectacle to see such a vast force collected in so lonely and forsaken a place. Selma about two hundred miles south on the Alabama river, a city of great importance to the rebels, was our first objective point. Our intention in the campaign was to find the cavalry corps of the rebel General Forrest and destroy it totally and forever, to burn and destroy all rebel government property, foundries, mills, rail roads, crops, &c., and in that way deprive Generals Lee and Johnston of munitions of war and provisions.

Every thing being carefully prepared, on the 19th of March, 1865, we began our magnificent campaign. We were well equipped. The men were armed with the Spencer carbine, and it was estimated that the whole expedition, the three divisions could fire over eighty thousand balls in a minute. Each one of our staff had three horses, and the escort of the staff was composed of one hundred picked dragoons. Some idea of the magnitude of our force can be conveyed to unmilitary minds by my stating that our division alone, when on the line of march, would cover a road equal in length to that from Cherry Valley to Lodi, over four miles.

On the 19th our wagon train moved ahead fifteen miles with an escort, out on the Goodloe road. After it had gone the general sent me to see if all was right. I started with an escort, and found

Commissary Brown in a dilemma, having his own mixed up with some of General McCook's wagons. I gave him some orders on my own responsibility, that would extricate him, and returned to headquarters, and reported to the general what I had done. On the evening of the 19th the 2d brigade and the battery moved out on the road fifteen miles, and on the 20th the 1st brigade and the headquarters cut loose from all means of communication with the north. As the 1st brigade moved across the river, cheers came to us from the fleet, and then the vessels turned their bows toward Nashville, and we our faces toward the Gulf. Our division was to have the advance for the first two hundred miles, and so we moved ahead of the rest of the corps.

Campaign of the Cavalry Corps, Military Division of Mississippi. March and April, 1865.

The first day's march carried us thirty-four miles from our starting point. Our headquarters were in the house of Mr. Thompson, a wealthy planter. During the day we had moved along and destroyed all we could of the Memphis and Charleston rail road. At three A. M. the hoarse sound of the bugle aroused the sleeping troopers. Contrary to our expectations none of us were very sore, and we congratulated each other, prematurely, as it afterwards appeared, upon our endurance. At the call, "boots and saddles," "to horse," we were in the saddles, and ready for thirty miles more. As we drew out I was surprised to see how long our division was, and thought we alone would be enough for Forrest, as was afterwards proved to be the fact. About noon I rode forward with the advance guard. There were signs of bushwhackers, and I was a little curious to see how those chaps looked in the west, but we saw none during the day. Towards evening, after a ride of thirty-two miles, our headquarters stopped for the night. The general left me at a cross roads to wait until General Alexander came up, to give him an order about his camps. I went into a house where there was a white woman, and about twenty negresses, more or less. I gave one of them a cigar, and the picture she made smoking it was very funny. Some of Alexander's advance went past, and she exclaimed with great earnestness, "O, de Lord, dare is two millions more Yankees." It was late before I was able to leave Alexander, and turning my horse's head I slowly rode to our headquarters. For twenty-five miles in our rear I could see the reflections of the thousands of camp fires of McCook and Long, the other two division commanders. At headquarters I found all but the sentinel in a deep slumber, and wrapping my long coat about me, was soon at rest. As on the day previous we awoke at three A. M., and as we got up to dress, the motions each one went through were comical enough to make one forget his own troubles. Never had my legs and knees been so stiff. After a breakfast on heavy biscuits we moved out and commenced the day's march. In the afternoon the advance met some guerillas, and had just enough firing to make the march interesting, and after the day was passed and the night orders issued, we were only too glad to lie down without dinner, and sleep through until the bugle would call us up. The first days of the march were tedious and void of excitement, though we were rapidly coming to a portion of the country where we would meet enemies, and where we expected to find valuable property belonging to the rebel government, which we intended totally to destroy. We had entered the great wilderness of northern Alabama, and for sixty miles rode on the crests of immense hills covered with pine woods. During the entire distance there were but two small creeks, the water in which was insufficient to satisfy the wants of our men and horses. Deer started up in our path, and gazing on us with their brilliant eyes, lightly bounded away. On the evening after a wearisome march of forty miles, we arrived at the Mulberry fork of the Black Warrior river, and then the troops went into camp, and satisfied their craving for water.

Crossing of the Mulberry.

Upon our reaching the river the general and I rode along it, to see how the division would cross. On either side the banks were rugged and steep, the stream was deep and rapid, and the bed rough and uneven. At a place where there had been a ford we thought we might cross, but upon trial, I discovered that the current was too strong for a horse to breast successfully. Upton tried it with the same result. We went further up the stream, and there found a more practicable crossing. The general was determined to put the troops over, even if he had to do so by leaving the trains and artillery in the rear to await the subsequent building of a bridge. We rode back to headquarters; Latta had been down to the river, and concluded that the job had better be turned over to some other division. I told him what was intended to be done, and we both agreed, the whole staff concurring, that as we would certainly be wet on the morrow, we had better take some "Pine top," in anticipation as a preventive to colds and rheumatism. Late at night leaving Green, who was an Irishman, expatiating on the Dublin medical college, we dropped asleep, and there remained until the unceremonious bugler sounded réveille. We then moved down to the river, and sent our escort on, who, after much difficulty, nearly all of them being unhorsed, reached the other bank. Then the 1st regiment was ordered forward, and as the men approached the river, I suppose they thought Upton must be a second Moses, if he could take them across that water in safety. The first squadron dashed in, the second followed; half the men slipped off their horses, and caught hold of their tails, the weight of the horses resisting the current, and this was the safest mode, if one did not mind the cold bath. Thus floundering and wading the division crossed in five hours, during which time many ludicrous incidents occurred. After all our dragoons were over, the trains and artillery were ordered up. The cannoneers knowing the bed of the river, were able to carry a considerable portion of the ammunition over in their hands. Each gun was drawn in the river by six horses, and on making the opposite side, six more were hitched on and drew the gun and the other six out. The trains were carried in the same way, the ammunition boxes being put up on sticks high in the wagon. By four P. M. not a vestige of the 4th division was on the north side of the river. But for the energy, perseverance and labor of General Upton, I doubt if we had crossed in as many days as hours. When General Wilson came to the river and saw where Upton had crossed, he gave him the highest praise, and said if Upton crossed, he must, and thereupon did cross, though with more trouble than we encountered. After we had moved a few miles our advance came to the Locust fork of the Warrior, a stream as large, but not so difficult to cross as the Mulberry. The same scene was acted as at the other river, and all passed over in safety.

The march was becoming very wearisome. On the 28th of March we entered Elyton, one hundred and fifty miles from Eastport, and made our headquarters with the Honorable Judge Mudd, confederate member of congress, where we stayed all day, and then left our honorable friend in somewhat straitened circumstances. Suddenly I was attacked by a violent high fever, and was considered to be in a fair way to die; but kind attention and cheerful spirits restored me, and I was in the saddle in a few days. While sick I rode in a carriage, politely taken from Mudd, and every mile thought of him as a benefactor. At Montevallo, skirmishing commenced with the advance of Roddy and Forrest, our skirmishers driving those of the enemy in first rate style, and forcing them back on their main lines at Plantersville.

Battle of Plantersville.

Plantersville was sixteen miles from and on the direct road to Selma, and by meeting us at this point, the rebels in a measure defended that city. As our advance was cautiously pushing its way towards Plantersville, it continually met the skirmishers of the enemy, until we were fairly upon the line of General Forrest. While quietly marching along, a shell came crashing over our heads, and soon we heard the sharp report of the carbines of our advance guard. The general and staff rode rapidly in front, to see the situation, and discovered that the whole rebel cavalry corps was before us. Forrest's lines were formed on hills in a semicircle, and in secure positions. Rodney's battery was in position, and doing its work well; Winslow's brigade was dismounted, and fighting on foot with the infantry of Forrest's command. Alexander's bugle rang out " By squadron into line," "Charge," and his brigade made a most gallant charge, driving all before it. General Winslow did the same thing with the infantry, and in half an hour General Forrest was in full retreat for Selma. During the battle which was a very brisk affair, General Upton so deported himself that he won the respect and admiration of the troops under his command. Mr. Keck's horse was killed, and Captain Gilpin's coat-tail was pierced by four balls. None of the staff were injured. General Wilson hearing the rapid heavy firing of the artillery in the fight hurried forward, and the day after the battle, the corps was concentrated, and moved as a corps upon Selma.

BATTLE OF SELMA, ALABAMA.

Sunday morning at day-light on the 2d of April, the corps was on the march; skirmishing commenced immediately as we advanced, and was steadily kept up all day, we having an advance sufficiently strong to drive all small bodies of the enemy before it. At 4 P. M., we were in sight of Selma. The city was defended by a complete line of powerful works forming a chain around its whole extent. The direction from which we came compelled us to pass over a plain, two miles in width, exposed to the enemy's artillery and musketry fire. In the town the church bells were tolling, and ministers in the streets exhorting the people to arm, and go out to the defenses, and each man to make it his ambition to kill a Yankee. At 6 P. M., our lines were formed for the charge, to take works manned by infantry, cavalry and fifty-six pieces of artillery. While General Long was forming his columns, he was forced to put out a strong skirmish line in rear to protect himself from the attack of bushwhackers and guerillas. Our division was placed on the right of the corps line, to charge mounted. At the order, the 2d division rushed like a whirlwind up to the works, and regardless of the destruction that was hurled through its ranks, jumped on the intrenchments, and half of Selma was won. The 4th division, led by Upton, in columns of squadrons, stormed the works in its front, and in half an hour after the attack was opened, Selma was in possession of the United States dragoons.

Some rebels tried to escape, but our division being mounted, captured nearly all. General Forrest, with an escort, and one or two other generals only escaped by swimming the Alabama river. Our division was in every street in the city; nothing could escape the vigilance of our troops. Every outlet of the city was barred, and in two hours after our victory, there were three thousand rebel prisoners in the stockade, which had been intended for our men when captured. At 10 P. M., our head-quarters were in an elegant house, a Mr. Johnston being our entertainer, and by twelve we were in beds as comfortable as if nothing unusual had happened.

The day after our occupation of Selma, we walked out to see the place. Being easy of access to the south, it was a great depot of supplies, and a place where all munitions of war were made. It was the most important city in the southwest, and one of the most important in the whole south. Parks, handsome residences, and fine broad avenues gave it a very aristocratic aspect. I learned that the three ministers, who were so anxious to have the Yankees killed, were all killed themselves. Blocks of six story buildings, filled with rebel government property, were set on fire by us, making for forty-eight hours a splendid, yet fearful conflagration. This work of destruction was complete.

While in Selma our staff had little else to do but walk about the ruined city. One day, Captain Gilpin and I met some ladies, with whom we had formed an acquaintance. In the favor of the prettiest one of these, I had flattered myself that I was ahead of Gilpin, but he completely flanked me on this occasion. When we joined them, the lady said to Gilpin, "Why does Captain Morse wear black (staff) shoulder straps, while yours are yellow" (cavalry)? "Oh," said Gilpin, "he commands a regiment of colored cavalry." That did the business for me with the Selma girls, thenceforth and forever.

The wagon train had been left so far behind that we were afraid lest some of the escaped troops of Forrest would destroy it, and therefore Alexander's brigade was ordered back towards Plantersville, to act as a guard. I went with Alexander, and, after a day's march of about twenty-five miles, met the train all safe. Taking an escort from the general, I rode forward towards Selma, which place I wished to reach several hours in advance of the brigade. On my way I met three or four of the blackest darkies I ever saw; with great delight they exclaimed, "Here comes our brudders."

As I returned to the city the main arsenal had just been fired. It was a building of the largest proportions, filled with all kinds of combustible materials, and made a fire truly fearful. A storm mingled its noise with that of the fire, and with both, Selma was a good representative of a warmer place. After a week passed in this city, every thing of importance in it was destroyed, and a great death blow of the rebellion in the southwest was struck by the United States. Arrangements were made to resume our march, and a pontoon bridge was laid across the Alabama river. The current being swift, and the bed of the river smooth, it was with difficulty that the bridge was kept together, as it was it was broken in several places while the troops were crossing, though no serious accident occurred. The trouble with the bridge so delayed the corps, that we were two days in reaching the opposite bank, but on the 10th of April the troops were in camp on the south side, waiting orders to move.

March to Montgomery.

Montgomery, the capital of the state, forty miles from Selma, was next to have the honor of our attentions. We expected a brisk encounter there, for though the place was of no great importance to us, its position was very advantageous for defense. We came in sight of the city at the end of the second day's march, and found that the advance had entered without opposition. The fortifications were too incomplete to warrant any attempt at defense, and therefore the rebels had evacuated the place, having first set fire to eighty thousand bales of cotton, which were burning as we entered the town, and having by other means, as they said, destroyed forty thousand more. We remained in Montgomery two days, and, of course, visited the capitol, where Jefferson Davis, and the so-called confederacy were inaugurated. Were it not that the place was so far from active war operations, it would have been the capital of the south, instead of Richmond. After fully recuperating the men and horses, we once more resumed the march.

BATTLE OF COLUMBUS, GEORGIA.

Columbus, Georgia, is one hundred miles from Montgomery, on the south side of the Chattahoochee river. It was a place of nearly equal importance to Selma, and we felt assured that it would be desperately defended. At the rate of twenty-five miles a day, we would reach the city in four days. The marching was hot and tedious. Every few miles we would meet some portion of the enemy, and a sharp little skirmish would ensue. On the afternoon of the 16th of April, we heard rapid musketry firing in the direction of our advance, which was composed of a large regiment. We, the staff, all started on the full gallop, and after ten minutes' rapid riding came in sight of Columbus. One glance showed us it was well defended. The rebels had retained possession of Gerard, a suburb of the town, on our side of the river, and surrounded it by massive works well manned. It commanded and covered all the bridges, and must be taken before we could enter the city. As we came in sight of the enemy they opened on our little party a severe artillery fire. We were on a bare hill, in full view of the rebels, and for fifteen minutes we sat on our horses, taking our chances of being torn to pieces, while the general made observations of the works. Away to our left we saw a line of skirmishers coming out on the full run; the manner they acted convinced us that no troops but veterans could conduct themselves with so much regularity, under the circumstances. After the general had fully satisfied himself respecting the enemy's position, we withdrew and waited for the division, which was two miles back, to come up. Our advance was deployed as skirmishers, and held the enemy in check. An aid was sent back to hurry up the division, and in half an hour Alexander arrived, and his troops placed in line of battle on the hills, in front of the rebel left. Winslow's brigade was moved to our left five miles, there to attack a part of the rebel works, which Upton considered to be the key of the whole. By an error of a staff officer (not one of ours), Winslow's brigade was not on the ground at the time ordered, so it was late before he was ready. His attack was to be made with his men dismounted. Alexander, with his brigade mounted, as soon as Winslow's commenced, was to charge and carry the works in his front, sweep in the rebel rear and secure the bridges, thereby cutting off all escape. General Wilson arrived and approved of General Upton's arrangements, and said if he wanted any help he would order up the rest of the corps, but Upton thought the 4th division was sufficient to gain a victory over all the troops opposed to us.

At eight o'clock P. M., General Winslow reported himself ready for the attack; we mounted our horses, part of the staff went with Alexander and the others with Winslow and Upton. I went with the latter. As the bugle sounded "forward," our line advanced, and the enemy immediately commenced firing. We had to charge down a little hill, through a small valley and then up a slight hill to the works. The artillery fire of the enemy did great execution, and their musketry fire was very accurate; but in spite of the savage reception our men met with, they could not be prevented from gaining the breast works, and driving the rebels out in the open field, where they surrendered at discretion. Alexander performed the part allotted to him, but not before two bridges had been fired; but there were still three left, and as they were taken they answered our purpose. After all our prisoners were under strong guards, and the affair was settled we sent three regiments across the river to Columbus, and placed the city under guard till morning.

The general and I were alone; none of the staff nor orderlies were to be found, being all busy in their different places. We thought we would go in a house and sleep until morning. Near the rifle pits was a large house up to which we rode.

I dismounted and gained admittance by kicking open the door. The place was deserted and I built a fire out of an old chair. The general remembered that he had seen a man in charge of the rebel General Buford's dinner, and I went for and captured the man and the dinner — both poor stuff. After dining we went to sleep. In the morning from the window I saw twelve hundred prisoners in a fort a few yards from the house. We rode across the bridge into the city and breakfasted at the hotel, and then I went out in search of a house for headquarters. We had captured thirty-five hundred prisoners, fifty pieces of artillery and large quantities of munitions of war. The commander of the rebel forces, General Howell Cobb, escaped and rode his horse ninety miles before he drew rein. There were more large buildings and more extensive magazines in Columbus than in Selma, though it was not so important a place. General Winslow was made military governor, and to him the duty of burning government property was assigned. Soon recurred horrible scenes of destruction; blocks and blocks burning and falling, shells bursting, and powder exploding made day and night hideous. Whole streets were burned. The fire at Selma was small compared to this. The demolition of every thing that could be of use to the rebels was complete, and in the destruction of Columbus and Selma, Generals Lee and Johnston were made to understand, that our expedition was not a mere raid, but that it alone was rapidly destroying the rebellion in its very vitals. The time we remained in Columbus was spent in resting the troops. Four hundred miles of incessant riding had greatly debilitated men and animals; but after some days when the weather had grown cooler, and when the glory of success had seemed to cover up the ragged clothes, orders for a move were issued. General Long's division took the lead and we the rear.

March to Macon, and News of Peace.

Macon, on the Ocmulgee, is one hundred miles from Columbus. All along on our way thither we found immense stores of provisions collected to be taken east for the rebel armies. We appropriated all we wanted for our own use, and destroyed the rest.

As yet, we had heard nothing from our army in the east, and were anxious to learn how General Grant had succeeded in the battles which we knew must have taken place. While on his way to Macon, and about twenty miles from there, General

Wilson received orders from General Sherman, forwarded by General Johnston through his lines, to cease raiding, and encamp his corps; but Wilson, before reading the despatch, sent his advance on to Macon, to demand its surrender. It was surrendered without a fight, and occupied by the 72d Indiana mounted infantry. During the day on which General Wilson received this order, the corps moved into the town. Our division was marched into East Macon, and there went in camp. Our headquarters were made in the house of a Mrs. Flanders. I did not cross the river with the staff, but came afterward, and on reaching the house saw our staff acting in the wildest kind of a way. Latta, especially, was performing the most athletic kind of tumbling. I enquired the cause of their joy, and learned that Lee had surrendered, and that the war was over. If General Grant has all the health we drank for him that night, there will not be a vacant lieutenant generalship by death for upwards of two hundred years. One of General Sherman's staff had come through the rebel lines, and informed us of the happy news. Soon we received the order from the secretary of war to fire two hundred guns in honor of victory. Rodney's battery was placed in position on hills above the city, and fired the salute. We could scarcely believe that the war was over; the news had come so unexpectedly, that we were not prepared for the joyful tidings. Our headquarters were moved up on a little hill overlooking East Macon. Macon is a city of eight or ten thousand inhabitants. It seemed to me, for the most part, a poor sort of place, with some good houses in it. It is essentially a representative southern town.

Outside of the city were the stockades where our soldiers had been so barbarously treated, and thirty miles off was the world-renowned hell on earth, that hideous comment on the spirit of slavery, Andersonville. While we were there one of Wilson's staff arrested Jeff. Davis's infamous and wretched tool, Captain Wirtz.

After two weeks passed in Macon, we were glad when General Wilson ordered General Upton to Augusta to demand the surrender of that place.

ATLANTA AND AUGUSTA.

My health for some time past had been failing, and now, as the war was over, I felt unable and unwilling to return with the division five hundred miles to Nashville. I went to General Wilson, and expressed to him my desire to leave the army, and requested a leave of absence that I might improve the first opportunity to go north. He very kindly gave me a leave for thirty days, with permission to apply for an extension. Giving orders for the division to follow by easy stages, General Upton and I went to Atlanta by rail, and reached there late at night, after traveling all day, at the rate of six miles an hour. The appearance of this town, after General Sherman's abode there, baffles my powers of description. It stood as a warning of the swift ruin which must come on all who may attempt to destroy our government. We learned there that Jeff. Davis was in the vicinity, and telegraphed the fact to General Wilson. The great criminal was soon afterwards arrested by Colonel Pritchard of the 2d division.

At midnight we took the cars for Augusta, about a hundred and fifty miles, and arrived there the next evening. Leaving our baggage at the hotel, we walked slowly up the streets, much to the disgust of the citizens, who had never seen Yankees there during the war, except as prisoners. Our escort, or guard of several hundred men, followed in command of their officers. At the Planter's Hotel, we engaged rooms and made arrangements to parole the troops of different rebel commands in that part of the country. The advent of a United States major general and staff, to demand the surrender of the place, and of the troops in the vicinity, created considerable excitement; but though every one looked their hatred, no one ventured to molest us. Up to this time, though we had heard rumors of the death of Mr. Lincoln, we had had no proof of the sad fact, but here upon the arrival of General Mollineaux from Savannah, we received the order for mourning, and put crape on our arms. A detachment of our troops was sent up to Albany to parole the division of General Debbill, which was composed of two brigades commanded by Generals Duke and Vaughn. These two latter generals came to Augusta and were paroled by us. General Duke afterwards went on to New York with me on his way home to Kentucky.

At this time we caused to be posted bills offering a reward for the apprehension of Jeff. Davis, and thereby caused great indignation and impotent threats from his whipped and broken down followers. On Sunday evening we mounted our horses, and rode about to see the city, and then crossed the Savannah to stand and gaze upon the precious and sacred soil of South Carolina. The result of our observations of place and people was, that though Augusta is by nature one of the loveliest places imaginable, we would rather be excused from dwelling long among such an ignorant, debased and hateful population as we met in the streets. A portion of General Mollineaux's brigade arrived from Savannah, and the city was placed under military control. As General Upton intended to return to Atlanta he gave the command of the place over to General Mollineaux. I made up my mind to go to Savannah and thence to New York.

LEFT ALONE. VOYAGE TO SAVANNAH.

The general and staff left me, and when they said their kind and affectionate farewell, and took the train to Atlanta, leaving me in the hotel to enjoy the society of about one hundred rebel officers, I felt rather disconsolate. I had to wait in Augusta five days before a steamer came up the river, and two or three before she was ready to return. At length the little boat, the Leesburg, was ready, and by order from General Mollineaux, I went on board before any others were permitted to go, and thereby secured proper accommodations. The boat was under the orders of a second lieutenant of the 19th corps, but as I was a staff captain, he was disposed to let me have a good deal to say in the management of affairs, and the responsibility

I was ready to assume, as we had a water captain to manage the boat.

I had the only state room, and invited to share it with me a lieutenant of the guard, a Mr. Wright, a Captain Somebody, formerly of Stonewall Jackson's staff, and old Commodore Tatnall, once of the United States, and later of the rebel Musquito navy. On board were about forty paroled rebel officers, twenty of our own guard, and four torpedoes looking ugly enough to blow us to pieces.

Alligators were sunning themselves all along the banks, but though constantly shot at, I saw only four killed.

After a voyage of two days down this beautiful river, on the evening of the second day we came in sight of the fair city of Savannah, and as the little boat reached the wharf, a crowd collected to learn the news from the interior. Leaving the loquacious part of the passengers to narrate the stirring events that were transpiring in Georgia, Mr. Wright and I took rooms at the house of a friend of his in the town.

Voyage to New York.

I remained in this beautiful city five days, and then obtaining a pass from General Grover, went by the little boat, U. S. Grant, to Hilton Head, there to take an ocean steamer to New York. The Arago, Captain Gladsen, was to sail the next day; and, accordingly, in the morning all the passengers assembled on board. As we were on the deck, the small steamboat, Cathara Clyde, came past, having on board a precious cargo, in the person of Jefferson Davis, and as we weighed anchor and moved off, she, I mean the boat, followed in our wake. The state rooms were chosen by rank, and as there were only three or four colonels among the passengers, and I was one of the ranking captains, I had one of the best. I had many acquaintances on board, and my friend, Captain Baker, whom I had known when he was on General Franklin's staff, was made adjutant of the ship. I had been selected for that office by the old colonel in command, but on my assuring him that as soon as we were at sea I would be unfit for duty, he excused me from the service, and made Baker the unlucky official. This was my first venture on the mighty deep, but I took it for granted that sea-sickness was hereditary in my family, and soon found to my sorrow that I was not mistaken. By a strict diet of lemons and claret I managed to keep tolerably steady till off Cape Hatteras, and then became oblivious of all things till we reached Fortress Monroe. Here we again saw Jeff. Davis, on the deck of his little boat, waiting for his casemate to be prepared for him.

After coaling, we steamed on, and in twenty-four hours saw the beach of New Jersey, and late Saturday night on the twenty-third of May, 1865, entered the harbor of New York.

It only remains for me to add, to close the recital of my connection with civil war, I trust forever, that in July, 1865, I was mustered out of the service, and that in August, 1866, I was honored by his excellency, Governor Fenton, with the brevet rank which is inscribed on the title page.

INDEX.

An Expedition of the 121st, 45.
An Escape, 95.
An Execution, 44.
Appointed Adjutant, 10.
Arrived at the Regiment, 8.
Arrived at Falmouth, 7.
A Red-headed Surgeon, 110.
A Scare, 9.
Atlanta and Augusta, 144.
At Louisville, Kentucky, 117.

Battle of Bleak Hill, 93.
Battle of Cold Harbor, 100.
Battle of Columbus, 137.
Battle of Gettysburg, 30.
Battle of Locust Grove, 59.
Battle of Plantersville, 131.
Battle of Rappahannock Station, 51.
Battle of Salem Chapel and Chancellorsville, 22.
Battle of Selma, 132.
Battle of the Wilderness, 76.
Black-burying, 77.
Burning of the Gult House, 119.
Burnside Relieved, 17.
Burnside's Move in the Mud, 14.
Burying the Dead, 104.

Campaign Abandoned, 63.
Campaign of the Cavalry Corps, M. D. M., 125.
Campaign of Chancellorsville, 20.
Campaign of Gettysburg, 30.
Campaign of Mine Run, 57.
Campaign of the Wilderness, 77.
Camp in Summer, 43.
Cherry Valley in Summer, 112.
Commissioned, 5.
Crossing the Mulberry, 128.

Dismissed the Service, 11.

Falmouth, 7.

General Bartlett's Ball, 72.
General Sedgwick killed, 83.
General Grant Appears. 74.
General Upton Wounded, and Change of Plans, 113.
General Wright appointed commander of 6th Corps, 83.
Guerillas, 44.

Hooker made General in chief, 17.

In Camp, May and June, 1863, 27.
Increased Carnage, 91.

Ladies in the Army 71; banished, 74.
Left Alone, 147.

Marching, 48.
March to Macon, 142.

March to Montgomery, 136.
March to the Pamunkey, 99.
Movement threatening Washington, 111.

Nashville, 117.

Organization of the Expedition, 121.
Our Dinner, 66.

Perils on the way to Louisville, 115.
Preparations for the Campaign of the Wilderness, 75.
Presentation to Gen. Meade, 66.
Presents and Punch, 69.
Promotion, 51, 117.
Pursuit of Gen. Lee, 39.

Rebel Trick detected, 90.
Restored to the Service, 13.
Return to the Army, 68.

Sickness and Kindness, 106.
Sneaking and Grubbing, 105.
Spottsylvania Court House, 88.
Started for the War, 5.

The Bloody Angle, 92.
Third Crossing of the Rappahannock, 29.

Upton's Brilliant Charge, 85.

Voyage to New York, 148.
Voyage to Savannah, 147.

Went Home, 67.
Winter Quarters of 1863 and 1864, 64.

www.ingramcontent.com/pod-product-compliance
Lightning Source LLC
Chambersburg PA
CBHW030333170426
43202CB00010B/1109